What School Boards Can Do

What School Boards Can Do

REFORM GOVERNANCE
FOR URBAN SCHOOLS

Donald R. McAdams

Foreword by Rod Paige

Teachers College, Columbia University
New York and London

Published by Teachers College Press, 1234 Amsterdam Avenue, New York, NY 10027

Library of Congress Cataloging-in-Publication Data

McAdams, Donald R.
    What school boards can do : reform governance for urban schools /
Donald R. McAdams ; foreword by Rod Paige.
        p.   cm.
    Includes bibliographical references and index.
    ISBN 0-8077-4648-7 (pbk. : alk. paper)
        1. Urban schools—United States—Administration.   2. School boards—United States.
    3. School improvement programs—United States.   I. Title.

    LC5141.M33 2006
    379. 1'531—dc22

                                                                        2005050662

ISBN-13: 978-0-8077-4648-6 (paper)   ISBN-10: 0-8077-4648-7 (paper)

Printed on acid-free paper
Manufactured in the United States of America

13   12   11   10   09   08   07   06   8   7   6   5   4   3   2   1

To America's urban school boards and their superintendents

Contents

Foreword

REFORM GOVERNANCE IS DESTINED to become the standard governance model for urban school boards and, perhaps, for all school boards. It is a fresh look at a complex subject by one of the nation's leading authorities on urban school boards. Based on rich experience and deep thought, this book by Don McAdams offers a governance theory that is more than best practices on how effective boards work; it is also a guide to what boards should be doing, namely, providing leadership for the redesign of urban districts.

McAdams has grasped the reality that urban districts as they have been organized and managed for more than a half century are not up to the job required in the 21st century. No longer is it acceptable to educate some or even most children. America must educate all its children to high levels, and urban districts, which disproportionately educate America's children of color and poverty, must be redesigned for this task.

In America, the 50 states have primary responsibility for education. And because the people of America want the federal government to play an increasingly important role in supporting standards and accountability, the Congress of the United States passed and President George W. Bush signed into law the No Child Left Behind Act. However, as one who has had the privilege of serving as a board member and superintendent in an urban district and as secretary of education of the United States, I can state unequivocally that as important as is the role of state and federal policy makers, neither state nor federal policy makers can redesign urban school districts. Only those leading urban districts can.

Board members, because they represent the people and have the power to act, and superintendents, because they have professional knowledge and the responsibility to lead and manage, are close enough to communities and schools to see what needs to be done and powerful enough to do it. They are the governance team. In this team, because of their link with the people and because they have the responsibility to select executive leadership and oversee the work of management, boards are the dominant partner. Working together as change agents, strong board-superintendent teams can and must redesign urban districts.

This book shows the way. It is a comprehensive theory of governance, described by a simple conceptual framework that encompasses all the work of a reform board. Everything is here: from big ideas about core beliefs and theories of action for change, to the fundamental relationships and processes by which boards and superintendents work together, to the leadership responsibility boards have to build community support for sustained change.

This volume is not a handbook that explains how everything is to be done. No governance model could do that. The work of boards is too contextual. Rather, the book puts forth principles as guides to action with enough examples to make them clear. Boards that keep these principles in mind as they struggle to improve student achievement in their districts will find them to be powerful tools.

After 11 years as a board member and superintendent in one of America's largest urban school districts, I thought I knew a lot about governance and reform leadership, but McAdams has taught me a few things I did not know, and he has laid out reform governance with such clarity that he almost makes reform leadership look easy. I can assure everyone that it is not. Still, I wish I had started my work as a board member in Houston with this book in my hand. The work would have been easier than it was, and I think we would have made more progress than we did.

—Rod Paige
Former U.S. Secretary of Education

Preface

FROM 1990 TO 2002, I SERVED on the Houston Independent School District Board of Education, in 1993 and 1997 as board president. During these years, especially during the superintendency of Rod Paige, 1994–2001, Houston made significant improvements in student achievement and district operations. The Broad Foundation recognized these improvements when it awarded Houston the inaugural Broad Prize for Urban Education in 2002.

The day the prize was awarded, Paige, who had served on the Houston Board of Education for 4 years before being named superintendent and was now U.S. secretary of education, called to give me the news. "Don, do you remember in 1990 when some of us on the board dreamed of making Houston the best urban district in America? Well, the good news is we did it. The bad news is, if Houston is the best, America's urban districts must be in terrible shape."

Indeed they are. Those who know Houston well know that the reforms of the Paige era have put down only shallow roots and without nourishment will wither away. The same can be said about other urban districts. There is evidence of improvement in America's urban districts, but on balance these districts are failing to educate far too many of the children they serve.

I am convinced that, second only to national security, the nation's highest priority should be educating all children to grade level or above and eliminating the achievement gap. This is not only a moral imperative; it is a necessity. To allow our nation to be divided into haves and have-nots risks our standard of living, quality of life, and even our democracy.

If this is to be done, it must be done in America's great urban school districts. States create the financial, organizational, and educational policy framework, and children are taught in schools. School districts, however, are the only units of government that can guarantee good schools for all children. Districts are the legal entities established by the states to educate children. They are the link between state policies and state funding and schools. They are the units that manage human resources, financial resources, facilities, and support services; and they create the policies that determine what happens in schools. Brilliant school principals willing to swim against the tide can create a few good schools in low-performing school districts. Only districts can create good schools for all children.

Some will argue that there are alternatives. Indeed, charter schools and vouchers offer immediate opportunities for children whom the public schools have failed. Over time the competition they offer may have a positive effect on urban districts. But now and for years to come, the overwhelming majority of children will be in traditional public schools. The quickest and most efficient way to provide good schools for all urban children is to improve these schools.

Who can do this? I am convinced that the most powerful agents for change are boards of education. On this point, I am at odds with most observers of urban education. Most believe that superintendents are the key and that school boards are barriers to reform.

Boards are charged with having a focus on everything but student achievement, micromanaging, and putting special interests and personal agendas ahead of the needs of children. Increasingly, major urban districts are coming under the control of mayors. When researchers, policy makers, and superintendents talk about reforming urban boards, they usually define reform as stripping boards of their power.

Sadly, some urban boards are dysfunctional. So are some other democratic institutions. This is no argument for eliminating them or stripping them of their power. Rather, it is an argument for showing them how to use their power to reform their districts. There are some positive examples. Everywhere an urban district has made significant improvements there has been a strong reform leadership team of board and superintendent.

Boards are powerful. They select; evaluate; and, if they choose, terminate superintendents. They set goals, allocate resources, create policy frameworks, and oversee management and are the bridge between districts and the publics they serve.

Boards govern, and rightly so. School districts are democratic institutions. In a democracy, the people must control their public institutions. Somebody or some body must exercise power on behalf of the people. Boards represent the people and are instruments of state government.

I believe that boards, whether they are elected or appointed, must be powerful. For only with power can they be effective change agents. Indeed, only boards, because of the power they derive from the people and their link with the people, have the mandate and the power to lead fundamental change.

This book is for boards that choose to do so. It is the distillation of my 12 years of experience on the Houston board, conversations with many of the most creative urban reform theorists and practitioners in America, oversight of the writing of a score of teaching cases on urban district governance for The Broad Institute for School Boards and other board-training institutes managed by the Center for Reform of School Systems, and my experience providing training to the boards of dozens of the nation's largest urban school districts.

What I have learned is that most boards are confused about their work. They are not certain what they are supposed to do and how they should do it. They are absorbed with little things and pulled into micromanagement, vexing their superintendents and undermining management systems. And the major processes by which they operate are inefficient at best and sometimes dysfunctional. Meanwhile, they fail to use the powerful governance levers placed in their hands to drive fundamental redesign of their districts. In short, they do not know how to govern as change agents for high performance.

What they lack is not talent or good intent, for on balance urban school board members, at least those I have known, are successful in their professional lives and care about children and public schools. What they lack is a comprehensive theory of governance that applies effective governance skills, in the hot political arena of urban education, to the task of redesigning urban school districts. This is reform governance.

Acknowledgments

THIS BOOK WOULD NOT HAVE BEEN POSSIBLE without the help of many friends. First I wish to thank the numerous school board members and superintendents with whom I have been privileged to work: both those in the Houston Independent School District, my original teachers, and the many from districts throughout America with whom I have worked as a board trainer and consultant. The names are far too many to mention. I hope they have learned half as much from me as I have from them.

I also wish to thank the many donors who have supported the work of the Center for Reform of School Systems, especially The Broad Foundation, The Houston Endowment, and The Meadows Foundation. Because of them, I have been able to oversee significant research on urban district leadership and work with scores of urban school board–superintendent teams.

Quite a few friends contributed directly to this book. Dan Katzir, Veronica Davey, Sarah Glover, and Michelle Wisdom helped me think deeply about governance, critiqued my ideas, and offered many excellent suggestions. Michelle also assisted with research and prepared all the graphics. Rick Hess and Anne Bryant offered valuable suggestions on points large and small, Richard Fossey critiqued my prose, and Betsy Breier assisted with formatting and proofreading.

Several of the nation's premier urban reform leaders have enriched the book with comments from their own experience. Only friendship can explain their willingness to provide such thoughtful and illuminating responses on such short notice. My gratitude goes to Alan Bersin, Joseph Olchefske, Tom Payzant, Gail Littlejohn, Ron Ottinger, Julian Treviño, and Susan Wilkinson.

My deepest gratitude goes to Sara Taggart, who is far more than a research consultant. She did extensive research; prepared the bibliography; and assisted with figures, tables, and formatting. Also, I want to thank my editors at Teachers College Press, Brian Ellerbeck and Wendy Schwartz. They have both deep knowledge about education and patience with authors, and they know how to turn a manuscript into a book.

Finally, my wife, Anne, on top of her deep commitment to our family and her profession, put up with my extensive travel and weekend writing, partially because she believes in my work, but mostly because she loves me. Thanks, Anne.

Notwithstanding all this help, this book still has many imperfections. And those who have helped do not necessarily share my point of view and no doubt disagree with some of my opinions. Everything—the viewpoint, the opinions, the mistakes, and the gaps in knowledge—are my responsibility, and mine alone.

Introduction

THIS BOOK IS FOR URBAN SCHOOL BOARD members who want to create high-performing school districts. In it I propose a comprehensive theory of board leadership for eliminating the achievement gap at high levels—what I call reform governance. I believe that superintendents, school administrators, business leaders, parent activists, and all who work with urban school boards will also find value in this book.

Reform governance builds on the excellent work of state school board associations, the National School Boards Association (NSBA), John Carver, and others (Carver, 1997, 2001, 2002; Carver & Carver, 1997). It embraces good governance practices and the principles of policy governance. Like the NSBA's *Key Work of School Boards Guidebook* (Gemberling, Smith, & Villani, 2000), which sets forth in powerful yet simple language the board's leadership responsibilities in the areas of vision, standards, assessment, accountability, resource alignment, climate, collaboration, and continuous improvement, it sees boards as change agents for student achievement and supports whole systems change.

Reform governance, however, does more than synthesize these approaches. It provides a conceptual framework that brings all the work of a reform board into a coherent whole, built around the belief that fine-tuning school districts as they presently exist will not achieve the results desired. Urban districts must be redesigned—and urban districts cannot be redesigned without the active leadership of school boards. Reform governance, in short, is governance for a purpose, not just governance as a process. It brings together process, urban district reform knowledge, and board leadership for the purpose of creating high-performing school districts.

Reform governance, reform boards, and *reform superintendents* are terms used throughout this book. *Reform,* according to Microsoft Word's online dictionary, means "reorganization and improvement of something, especially a political institution or system that is considered to be faulty, ineffective, or unjust." Reform boards and superintendents are boards and superintendents committed to transforming ineffective urban districts into high-performance organizations that will eliminate the achievement gap at high levels. Reform governance is what and how they do it. The elements of reform governance are presented in a conceptual framework in Chapter 2 and explicated in the rest of the book.

In Chapter 1, I assert the central role of school districts in the education of children and the inadequacy of the prevailing model, designed nearly 100 years ago, to meet the needs of the 21st century. Nothing less than the fundamental redesign of school districts is required. I then affirm the imperative for strong superintendent leadership, touch briefly on the democratic roots of school board authority, and introduce the challenging yet essential partnership between boards and superintendents.

Clarity on the difference between governance and management and the roles and responsibilities of boards and superintendents is at the heart of reform governance. This theme is introduced in Chapter 1 and developed throughout the book as the various elements in the Reform Governance Framework are presented.

Chapter 2 provides an overview of reform governance. I explain the Reform Governance Framework and the dynamic relationship of the parts to the whole. Each one of the elements in the framework, corresponding to a major sphere of board action, is described. The elements are core beliefs and commitments; theories of action for change; roles, responsibilities, and relationships; building blocks of reform governance; policy development and oversight; policies to transform urban districts; civic capacity; and transition planning.

In Chapters 3 through 9, I develop these elements, starting with core beliefs and commitments in Chapter 3. The point of this chapter is that, notwithstanding that the achievement gap is deeply rooted in America and the school effect is not 100 percent, urban boards should commit themselves to eliminating the gap at high levels. There are good reasons to believe this can be done; and if it is to be done, school boards will have to lead the way.

In Chapter 4, I ask the question, What must a board do to eliminate the achievement gap? The reform governance response is that school districts as they have been traditionally organized and operated, no matter how well funded or managed, cannot educate all children to high levels. They were not designed for this purpose. New designs are required.

The core of Chapter 4 is a description and analysis of three comprehensive theories of action: managed instruction, performance/empowerment, and managed performance/empowerment. Since the mid-1990s, innovative board-superintendent teams have been acting on these still-developing theories of action to redesign their districts, and with encouraging results. The chapter includes examination of several district redesigns.

The reader should note that these references to school districts are strokes with a broad brush. Large urban districts have such variety within them and are so resistant to change that almost no generalization about them is totally accurate. What district leaders say is happening may be happening only infrequently in a few places. Nevertheless, from a high altitude, one can see clear differences among school districts and over time chart different trajectories.

Chapters 3 and 4 feed directly into Chapter 8, for a commitment to high performance and clarity on what is needed to achieve it provide the imperative and the outline for transformational policies. Something more is needed, however. Before boards can be effective policy makers, they and their superintendents must be able to work together as high-performance teams. This means clarity on roles and responsibilities and productive relationships, the subject of Chapter 5; effective processes for board work, the subject of Chapter 6; and policy-making skills, the subject of Chapter 7. Whereas Chapters 3 and 4 focus more on *what*, Chapters 5–7 focus more on *how*.

In Chapter 5, I examine the two major issues that most frequently lead to conflict between boards and superintendents: constituent service and management oversight. Boards have a democratic responsibility to provide constituent service and a fiduciary responsibility to oversee management. Unfortunately, constituent service can all too easily become problem solving and favor seeking, and management oversight can all too easily become management by the board. In Chapter 5, I recommend best practices for effective constituent service and management oversight without micromanagement.

In Chapter 6, I recommend best practices for board meetings, board workshops, and board committees. Boards act as a body, not as individuals. Workshops as tools for management oversight and to drive a reform agenda; the proper use of standing and ad hoc committees and committees of the whole; and focused, professionally run, productive business meetings are the essential processes by which boards do their work.

Policies crafted to advance a theory of action and make possible the achievement of performance goals should be the primary work product of a board. Policy leadership requires deep knowledge of policy development methods and principles and effective policy oversight. In Chapter 7, I introduce this body of knowledge, explain the difference between routine operating policies and reform policies, and show boards how to exercise policy leadership.

In Chapter 8, I put forward in abbreviated form major policies that derive from the comprehensive theories of action presented in Chapter 4. These policies, implemented effectively and in proper alignment, are those that current practice indicates have the power to transform urban districts. Whereas Chapters 5–7 provide guidance on how boards committed to high achievement can most effectively do their work, in Chapter 8 I outline the work that needs to be done.

A reform board's work does not end with effectively implemented reform policies. Because boards are instruments of democracy and because creating a new district structure and culture requires constancy of purpose over a decade or more, two important jobs remain. Boards must build broad public support for deep and ongoing reform and prepare for the changes in leadership that will inevitably occur. In Chapter 9, I cover this work.

Finally, in Chapter 10, the conclusion, I briefly review the elements of reform governance, outline the major design principles that I believe will characterize urban districts of the future, and restate my case that without reform leadership by boards of education, urban districts cannot and will not be redesigned. The big unknown is not what school boards can do; it is whether Americans will demand high-performing school districts and elect board members who can and will do what needs to be done.

CHAPTER 1

Why Boards Must Lead

WHO IS IN CHARGE of America's urban schools? Everyone and no one. We Americans love divided government. Distrustful of power, we established a constitution with three branches of government, each designed to check the power of the others.

We have done the same thing with our schools. What could be more important than our children? Who can we trust to be in charge? We have diffused power over schools to state legislatures, to school districts, to the federal government, to state and federal courts, and de facto to education professionals and teacher unions. Diffused power is great for preserving stability; it makes change almost impossible.

No center of power stands alone. Education reform requires systemic alignment. In the long run, state legislatures are in control. They make the laws and provide resources. Legislatures can create a framework and, most of the time, keep things from happening, but it is difficult for them to make things happen. Among the centers of power, school districts are the units that can most powerfully and quickly create good schools for all children in a community.

SCHOOL DISTRICTS

Until recently, most educational reformers overlooked school districts. The focus was on state policy and schools. School finance, state standards and accountability systems, state regulations of teacher preparation and compensation, whole-school design, curriculum, professional development, classroom management, and so on—these were the keys to improving student achievement.

The work of the past decade is substantial. The nation is now focused on improving schools, especially urban schools. State policy frameworks are far more focused and robust than 10 years ago and, thanks to the No Child Left Behind (NCLB) Act, are likely to become more so. We have a rich literature on teaching and learning, professional development, school performance, and a growing number of examples of high-performing urban schools. Nevertheless, improvements in student achievement are minimal, especially at the high school level, and the achievement gap remains large and almost unchanged.

In recent years, researchers and policy makers have realized they must turn their attention to school districts, especially large urban districts. These districts educate a disproportionate number of American children, particularly children of color and those from low-income backgrounds. Sixty-four of America's urban districts, those districts that are members of the Council of the Great City Schools, compose less than 1% of all districts but enroll 15% of the nation's public school children and about 32% of the nation's English-language learners. Nearly 70% of the students in these districts are African American or Hispanic, and 62% are eligible for free or reduced-price lunch (Council of the Great City Schools, 2002).

Most of these districts are in crisis. In 2003, only 48% of fourth graders in America's central city schools demonstrated at least basic mastery of reading on the National Assessment of Educational Progress (NAEP), with some urban districts registering rates as low as 31%. This is compared with 62% of fourth graders nationwide (NAEP, 2003). By the time these students reach high school, many are struggling to stay engaged and do not succeed. Graduation rates consistently paint a bleak picture for America's largest urban districts, where too often fewer than 50% of ninth graders graduate from high school 4 years later (Balfanz & Letgers, 2004; Swanson & Chaplin, 2003).

What is required to transform these districts into high-performing organizations that educate all children to high levels? The research base is still thin, but increasingly, researchers can identify the characteristics of a high-performing school district. And districts such as Houston, Long Beach, Garden Grove (California), Norfolk, Boston, Charlotte-Mecklenburg, and Aldine (Texas) have shown that entire districts, not just schools, can significantly improve student achievement. Where this has been done, district leadership has acted to redesign the system.

David Tyack's (1974) classic history of urban education, *The One Best System,* has given a name to the prevailing design of urban districts, a design created by administrative progressives in the early decades of the 20th century to Americanize the children of immigrants and prepare children for jobs in the American workplace. The workplace of about 1920 needed mostly skilled and unskilled labor. The public schools obliged. Following the principles of scientific management, administrative progressives adapted the factory model to educate and sort children for the workplace.

Just as manufacturing was standardized and consolidated, so was education. Children were grouped by age; learning was measured by hours of instruction; and children were sorted into college prep or vocational tracks, based all too often on gender, class, and race. Small school districts were consolidated into larger ones, and professional educators assumed responsibility for management. Governance was placed in the hands of smaller boards of education, elected on nonpartisan ballots in special elections and disproportionately representing the city's elite.

Much has changed since the 1920s. As have other public institutions, urban districts have evolved to keep pace with changing demographics, public values, social norms, business methods, and educational research; and there have been huge variations in time and place. Still, much has remained the same.

Most school districts still group children by age, assign them to classes, and move them lockstep through the traditional school day and year. Instruction is not designed to bring all children to standard; rather, children are given the opportunity to learn as much as they can in the time allotted and then moved on to the next subject or grade. Schools are the units of instruction, with little collaboration among schools. In many cases, teachers are free to close the doors to their classrooms and teach what they want, how they want. School districts manage schools in geographic areas, within which they have a monopoly on public education. Central Office assigns children to schools based on geographic attendance boundaries, assigns teachers based frequently on seniority, allocates resources based on staffing patterns, and controls school operations. Principals are middle managers who carry out Central Office directives under the supervision of assistant and deputy superintendents. And Central Office manages a massive business infrastructure, which provides the full range of business services to schools (Cuban, 1993; Cuban & Tyack, 1995; Mirel, 1999; Ravitch, 2000; Ravitch & Vinovskis, 2000; Stone, 1998).

However well the one best system met the needs of industrializing America, it was at root immoral, for it discriminated against girls, poor children, and children of color. It may have met the civil rights standards of the 1920s. It does not meet the civil rights standards of today.

And it no longer meets the needs of the workplace. Good jobs in today's global information economy require high school and more. Today's districts must educate all children to high levels, not only because it is the right thing to do, but also because it is essential for our economy and our democracy.

The 20th-century model cannot do this. No matter how well it is managed, no matter how much it is fine-tuned, the 20th-century model will not educate all children to high levels. It was not designed for this purpose. What is needed, and what is being attempted in the most successful urban districts, is fundamental redesign of the system.

SUPERINTENDENT LEADERSHIP

Clearly, superintendents alone cannot transform urban districts, but everywhere districts have improved, strong superintendents have pushed comprehensive reform agendas. For this reason, and also because executive leadership is highly visible, many see superintendents as the key to urban school reform.

Researchers have given considerable attention to the leadership role of superintendents and the obstacles that impede their ability to improve districts. High on the list of obstacles are school boards (Glass, Bjork, & Brunner, 2000). Not surprisingly, one of the two major strategies used in the past decade to improve executive leadership is to place districts under the control of mayors. Superintendents accountable to boards appointed by mayors are thought to have greater freedom to exercise executive power. The other strategy is to appoint nontraditional superintendents with strong executive backgrounds in business or the military.

Is executive leadership critical? Absolutely. Superintendents are the people who lead school districts, just as generals are the people who command troops and fight wars. Reform boards are helpless without reform superintendents.

DIRECT AND INDIRECT DEMOCRATIC CONTROL

The opposite is also true. Reform superintendents cannot succeed without reform boards—or reform governance power in whatever form it takes—standing behind them. In the successful districts mentioned above, all led by strong reform superintendents, strong reform boards worked as partners with the superintendent. This issue, the relationship between boards and superintendents, is at the heart of urban school reform.

We live in a democracy, and in a democracy the people must control their public institutions. We accomplish this by direct and indirect democratic control. We directly elect some executives: the president, governors, mayors, and so on. These elected officials, assisted by appointed officers, manage. They also govern, but their governance power is shared with legislative and judicial bodies. This is the American system of checks and balances.

We control other institutions through indirect democratic control. Elected officials appoint boards, which in turn appoint executives. For example, governors appoint university boards of regents, which in turn select university presidents.

Most school districts operate under direct democratic control; an elected board appoints the superintendent and has budget authority, some taxing authority, and ownership and responsibility for facilities and everything else. Although constrained by federal and state law, the board is the trustee for the people and directly governs the district. In many districts, boards share some governance power—especially budget and taxing authority—with city councils or other local elected bodies, and in some districts board members are appointed.

Even in districts where the board is appointed, however, board members are usually expected to pay close attention to parents and other constituents and have the final say on district policies. By design, legislatures have placed school districts as close as possible to the people they serve.

However we govern our schools, three points are clear: Governance springs directly or indirectly from the people; governance is always shared; and governance must control management. This is because our democracy has been designed to reflect the will of the majority, protect the rights of the minority, and check the exercise of power.

SCHOOL BOARDS AND SUPERINTENDENTS

School boards and superintendents are partners, but they are not equal partners. Boards govern. Superintendents manage. Governance always trumps management. Governance is the trusteeship of power on behalf of the owners of power; management is the exercise of power under the oversight of governance.

Governance is difficult to define, which is one reason there is so much confusion about it. That is why I have written this book, to provide an extended definition of governance for reform school boards. Simply put, governance is steering; management is rowing. Governance is deciding what is to be done; management is doing it. In a democracy, governance must be broadly shared. Management responsibility needs to be concentrated in individuals.

School boards govern; superintendents manage. But school boards do not govern alone. They share the powers of governance with state legislatures, the federal government, and the courts. The superintendent, because of his or her involvement in policy development, is also part of the governance team, though in a subordinate role. The board of education is the dominant partner in governance.

The board has the responsibility to establish core beliefs, create the vision, set goals, formulate a theory of action for change, direct and participate in the development of policies, approve policies, allocate resources, oversee policy implementation and the effectiveness of management systems, mediate between the district and the public, and look far into the future. To the extent boards abandon these responsibilities to superintendents, they cede their governance power.

Superintendents assume governance power for many reasons: because their boards lack the knowledge or the will to exercise it, because they believe they must combine governance and management power in order to effect change, or because they seek power for its own sake. For whatever reason, it is a mistake.

Indeed, many reform voices urge the concentration of power in the hands of superintendents. The move to mayoral control of urban districts happens not just because policy makers believe education is integral to the success of a city and must be aligned with the other functions of city government; it occurs also, perhaps primarily, because policy makers believe that elected boards bring personal and special interest agendas to the board table, micromanage, and make it almost impossible for superintendents to manage.

Sadly, this is often the case, and one of the reasons such cities as New York, Chicago, Philadelphia, Detroit, Cleveland, and Boston, to name some of the most well-known cities with appointed boards, have chosen this governance model. Indeed, Boston superintendent Thomas Payzant confirms:

> One of the qualities that attracted me to work in Boston was that a school board appointed by the mayor meant that the "stars were in alignment" and that I would be able to focus on instructional reform rather than political issues. (Personal communication, January 3, 2005)

It is universally recognized that in crisis situations power needs to be concentrated. Given the condition of many urban districts, concentrating power in the hands of a powerful superintendent such as Tom Payzant makes sense. It also makes sense to coordinate the services provided to children. Management, however, is not governance. Whether the governance is in the hands of the mayor, as it is in effect in New York and Chicago; an appointed board, as it is in Philadelphia; or an elected board, governance power should not be given to the superintendent. Concentrated executive power, yes; governance power, no.

No city can allow one person to establish core beliefs, create a vision, set goals, formulate a theory of action for change, develop a policy framework, and so forth. These decisions must reflect the community, and they cannot be changed every time a new superintendent comes to town. Imagine establishing new policies regarding magnet schools, charter schools, outsourcing, district accountability systems, funding formulas, variable or merit pay, and personnel evaluations every time a new superintendent came to town. No district can change course every 3 or even every 10 years.

All superintendents are transitional. Most urban superintendents are from out of town. They come for a season to provide executive leadership, and then move on, serving only 5 years on average (Glass et al., 2000; Natkin et al., 2002). Only with good fortune can a city keep a strong superintendent for the 10 or more years required to transform a district's systems and culture. Boards, whether elected or appointed, reflect the needs and culture of their community; and because they are likely to turn over a few members at a time, they provide structure and policy stability.

The almost revolutionary changes required to redesign urban school districts are not just management changes. They cannot be accomplished in a few years, and they cannot be accomplished without broad community support. Only boards, because of the democratic power they derive from the people, because of their close links with the people, and because of their stability, can provide the leadership required to redesign and sustain over decades school districts that provide equity and results for all children.

That most have not chosen to do so is not an argument for stripping them of their power. Rather, it is an argument for showing them how to exercise their power. The failure of urban boards is really the failure of democracy. The cure is not the diminution of democracy; it is the renewal of democratic power.

Nothing stated so far is intended to justify the dysfunctional behavior and lack of reform leadership on the part of many urban boards or to weaken the power of superintendents. Indeed, reform boards need strong superintendents—the stronger, the better.

As American Enterprise Institute scholar Frederick M. (Rick) Hess, one of the nation's leading authorities on school boards, puts it:

Reform boards that try to work through cautious, skeptical, or unenthusiastic superintendents are trying to row against the tide. District leadership will prove balky enough, even with a committed superintendent. Trying to drag along a large, bureaucratic organization and its top executives is a task beyond the ken of even the most effective reform board. (Personal communication, December 21, 2004)

Under the best of circumstances, the urban superintendency is not a job for the weak, unfocused, or indecisive. Only the best and brightest are likely to be successful reform superintendents. Strong boards do not imply weak superintendents. Power is not a zero-sum game.

What districts need are strong reform board–superintendent teams: boards that provide leadership for reform through vision, goals, policy, and astute politics; and superintendents empowered to manage for excellence. In this partnership, the superintendent will do most of the work. He or she is the chief executive officer and the only person who can create a new organizational culture. The board, however, will do the most important work, for governance makes possible management, not the other way around.

Julian Treviño, board president in the San Antonio Independent School District, puts it this way:

Boards have ultimate responsibility, for boards choose superintendents, not the other way around. Selecting a superintendent is the most important decision a board makes. Knowing the work that needs to be done, reform boards select the strongest reform leader they can find: the stronger the superintendent, the stronger the board. (Personal communication, December 24, 2004)

Creating high-performance urban school districts that educate all children to high levels should be the nation's number one educational priority. Without strong superintendents and strong boards working together to re-design urban districts, this cannot be done. Reform governance describes this work.

CHAPTER 2

Reform Governance:
An Overview

REFORM GOVERNANCE IS A COMPREHENSIVE THEORY of governance for urban school boards committed to effective and efficient district operations, high achievement for all children, and the elimination of the achievement gap. It is built on the belief that to achieve this outcome, urban districts must be redesigned.

To act, boards must be clear about their core beliefs and commitments. They must have a clear theory of action for change that drives redesign of their district through the enactment and oversight of aligned reform policies. Policy development and approval and all their other work must rest on clear and shared understandings of roles and responsibilities and board conventions about how work is done. And broad public support must be earned and continuity assured. These are the elements of the Reform Governance Framework (Figure 2.1).

Each box in the framework represents a board responsibility. Linked together, these responsibilities constitute the work of the board. Two major characteristics of the framework are the heavy horizontal line that indicates the division between governance and management—with the up and down arrows indicating that board members have no management authority but the superintendent is part of the governance team—and the arrows that link the elements above the governance/management line, indicating a conceptual flow from core beliefs to transition planning. The Reform Governance Framework brings together the full range of board thought and action and shows the relationships among all of the parts.

A conceptual framework, of course, is not reality. In the lives of board members, everything is happening at the same time. Nothing comes first and nothing comes last. There are no clear boundaries between any of the elements in the framework. And the governance/management line is wavy and moves. No static, two-dimensional model can describe reality. Nevertheless, theory guides the understanding of reality and makes possible the management of change.

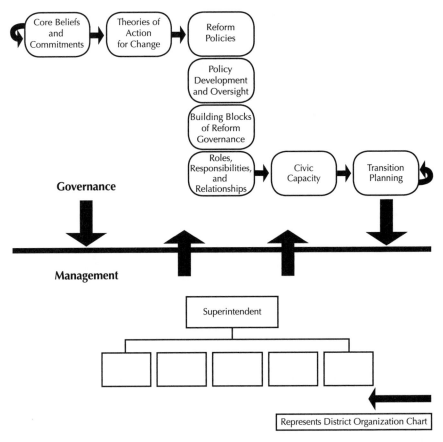

Figure 2.1. Reform Governance Framework.

CORE BELIEFS AND COMMITMENTS

The box at the top left of the framework in Figure 2.1 represents the board's core beliefs and commitments. This is the conceptual starting point for the work of the board: What do board members believe about children and America's public schools, and what are their commitments? Every board member should ask him- or herself the big question, Am I satisfied with incremental improvements in the status quo, or am I profoundly dissatisfied by the status quo and determined to change it as quickly as possible? One answer leads to governance as oversight; the other leads to governance as leadership for change.

Given the academic-achievement gap between middle-class and poor children and the achievement gaps between White and Asian children as compared with African American and Hispanic children, few boards should be satisfied with incremental improvements in the status quo. Every urban board member should be a change agent.

To be effective change agents, board members must have at least the following core beliefs and make the following commitments. They must believe that the 95% or so of children who do not have severe learning disabilities (hereafter in this book all children) can perform at grade level and graduate from high school with an academic diploma. They must believe that the school effect is significant and that school districts can become high-performing organizations. And they must commit themselves to grade-level performance and achievement to potential for all children and the elimination of the achievement gap.

These beliefs and commitments may sound utopian, but sufficient evidence exists to persuade us that with time and focused use of resources, all are achievable. Faith in ultimate success drives all successful human enterprises against great odds. Boards that do not share these beliefs and accept responsibility for these outcomes are not likely to succeed.

Gail Littlejohn, president of the Dayton, Ohio, school board, states her commitment this way: "By failing to rise above complacency and committing to all children learning, boards fail the test of leadership and let down the children and citizens who knowingly or not are relying on them to provide a bright future" (personal communication, February 2, 2005). Adds San Antonio's Treviño: "What is the purpose of serving if you're not committed to high achievement for all children?" (personal communication, December 24, 2004).

THEORIES OF ACTION FOR CHANGE

Beliefs and commitments lead to action, but what actions by a board will create a high-performing district? A board must have a theory of action for change, represented by the second box in the framework (see Figure 2.1). Clarity on a theory of action provides the foundation for goal setting and a strategic plan. Most important, a theory of action dictates the policy framework and guides the development and oversight of aligned reform policies. Policy leadership is one of the three most powerful levers for change placed in the hands of a school board—the others being superintendent selection and the bully pulpit.

A theory of change is a set of beliefs about how the world works. In the school reform context, a theory of change encompasses beliefs about how children learn, the motives that drive adult behaviors, the conditions that create organizational excellence, and the interplay between American democracy and democratic institutions. A theory of action for change is a set of beliefs about what actions by the board will create the desired changes. For example, a board that believes strongly in the effectiveness of command and control will create a policy framework that is very different from that of a board that believes strongly in collaboration or the power of the marketplace.

Most boards lack a clear theory of action, and for many with an implied theory of action, the theory is partial rather than comprehensive. Boards must understand that silver bullets will not fix urban districts. Shared-decision-making committees, small classes, small schools, alternative certification of teachers, pay for performance, public school choice, whole-school design, and other popular reform ideas may be parts of comprehensive theories of action, but alone they are likely to accomplish little. Boards must understand whole-systems change and seek comprehensive theories of action to change the whole system. Fortunately, some districts have pioneered comprehensive theories of action that hold great promise for districtwide high performance.

ROLES, RESPONSIBILITIES, AND RELATIONSHIPS

Policy leadership is the primary work of a board, and policy content is the primary output of a board's work. This work rests on an infrastructure that includes productive relationships between the board and superintendent, effective board meetings and other major processes by which the board does its work, and the correct application of the methods and principles of policy development and oversight. The stacked boxes that support the reform policy box in Figure 2.1 represent these elements.

Board members have numerous and complex relationships: with parents and other citizens, business and community leaders, elected officials, representatives of special interest groups, vendors, the superintendent, other district employees, and, of course, one another. Of all these, the most important are the relationships board members have with one another and with the superintendent. The box at the base of the vertical column in Figure 2.1 represents these relationships and the roles and responsibilities that come with them.

District reform is impossible unless the board and individual board members work in close partnership with a reform superintendent. The most powerful, focused, and capable board cannot reform a school district by working around an ineffective superintendent. A reform board must have a reform superintendent. And the board members and superintendent must have a common understanding of their roles and responsibilities. All too often, they don't. Board members cross the line into management, and superintendents assume the powers of governance.

Board members must provide constituent service. All elected officials do, and appointed board members no less than elected board members must intervene when constituents are not provided the service that policy requires. But there is a right way and a wrong way to serve constituents. Board members micromanage when they insert themselves into management decisions—about personnel, facilities, student discipline, or whatever. Micromanagement sows confusion, disrupts management systems, and weakens the superintendent's control of the district. By so doing, it diminishes the power of the board to govern. A weak superintendent cannot effectively implement the board's policies or be held accountable for the management failures of the system.

In the Reform Governance Framework, as seen in Figure 2.1, the dark horizontal line represents the line between governance and management. Note that the down arrows do not penetrate the line. This represents one of the most important principles of effective governance: Board members or the board as a whole should never cross the line into management.

Recognizing this principle, states Dayton's Littlejohn, "is the first major step in effective governance. It establishes the proper relationship between board members and the superintendent, enabling the superintendent to effectively manage and the board to hold the superintendent accountable for effective management" (personal communication, February 2, 2005).

Note, however, that the up arrows do penetrate the line. This represents the fact that the superintendent is part of the governance team. The board governs by policy, but it cannot make good policy without the superintendent. All policy affects budgets or personnel; all policy should be evaluated for effectiveness; and most policy development requires some technical expertise.

Even the most knowledgeable board does not have sufficient knowledge of the system to predict the impact of policies on budgets, personnel, and children. For these reasons, the superintendent must be part of the governance team. However, governance is not the responsibility of the superintendent; it is the responsibility of the board.

BUILDING BLOCKS OF REFORM GOVERNANCE

Board meetings, workshops, committees, and the structure and process by which board members deliver constituent services are the major processes by which the board does its work. The second box in the vertical column of the framework represents these building blocks of reform governance (see Figure 2.1).

Board meetings are the time and place at which boards act, and what the public sees at board meetings determines largely what the public thinks about the board. The keys to an effective board meeting are an agenda-review process that gives board members an opportunity to understand issues and raise questions; a short meeting that bundles routine items into one motion and focuses attention on a few major items, especially items relating to student achievement; and minimal participation by the public. Public comment is best received at public hearings following a board meeting or at hearings posted for the purpose of receiving input on a specific subject.

Workshops provide boards with an opportunity to educate themselves and the public and drive an agenda. Standing and ad hoc board committees can be effective vehicles for bringing action items to the board or they can be bottlenecks that encourage micromanagement.

Finally, board members have much constituent service and community-building work. This work can be done effectively only in partnership with the superintendent and requires unambiguous protocols and effective administrative support.

POLICY DEVELOPMENT AND OVERSIGHT

The third box in the vertical column in the framework shown in Figure 2.1 represents policy-development methods and principles and policy oversight. Perhaps 90% of all policies are routine operating policies, policies needed to enable the system to cope with changes in the environment. These policies may be driven by events that lead to unfavorable publicity or demonstrate systems failures, new technologies, changing demographic patterns, budget needs, and other factors. Some originate in the superintendent's office. Some bubble up through the organization.

These policies normally come to the board as superintendent recommendations, and the board has little if any involvement in their development, though if they are controversial—for example, school-attendance boundary changes—they may consume a great deal of the board's time. Boards should avoid spending time on routine operating policies, but they should be deeply involved in the development of reform policies, policies designed to change the district in fundamental ways to improve student achievement and district operations.

There are four major methods for policy development. Most routine operating policies come directly from the superintendent. Sometimes, because these issues are controversial or benefit from broad input, the superintendent charters a community task force to bring forward a recommendation. Board committees or task forces chartered by the board may also bring forth recommendations. Each method has advantages and disadvantages.

However the policy is developed, two principles apply. The policy should focus on ends, not means. And it should be only as specific as necessary to obtain results, allowing management as much freedom as possible to fill in the gaps. The more that policies add *how* to *what*, the more the board ties the hands of management, with numerous negative consequences.

Boards cannot assume that policies will be effectively implemented. Reform policies, especially, are likely to generate significant internal resistance. For all major policies, boards should set out how implementation will be measured and reported.

Implementation is not enough. Policies must work. Sometimes policies, however well implemented, do not achieve desired results. All major reform policies must be periodically evaluated. Again, along with requirements for reports on implementation, policies should contain requirements for evaluation.

POLICIES TO TRANSFORM URBAN DISTRICTS

The top box in the vertical column in Figure 2.1 represents properly aligned reform policies to transform urban districts. Reform policies should be enacted to advance the board's theory of action. The board must understand whole-systems change so that reform policies are properly aligned. For example, a board with a strong commitment to accountability for results would not want to adopt policies with heavy process-compliance requirements. Also, the order of policy implementation is important. Accountability policies, for example, should be implemented ahead of empowerment policies.

The primary work of a reform board is developing and approving reform policies. These policies advance the board's theory of action for change and in proper alignment will, over time, transform the structure, incentives, and culture of the district. Boards do many other things that are extremely important, but policies are the instruments by which they transform districts.

To be effective in the policy arena, board members must read widely in reform literature, become knowledgeable about what is working and not working in other districts, be clear about their theory of action for change and how the policies they are enacting support it, and be master politicians. And always, they must pay attention to their key relationships, especially those with one another and the superintendent, and the major processes by which they do their work.

BUILDING CIVIC CAPACITY

Even the most powerful board working with a strong reform superintendent cannot effect sustained change without the support of the community. Civic capacity for change is required. Flowing to the right of the Roles, Responsibilities, and Relationships box in the framework is a box representing the board's relationship with the people it serves and its responsibility to build civic capacity.

Schools are rooted deeply in the communities they serve. The public owns them, and it directly or indirectly chooses the board of education. Everyone is for better schools, but change threatens many special interests. A board-superintendent team that gets too far in front of the public it serves will find itself without support. And when broad public support is absent, special interest groups will kill bold reform policies, and reform will grind to a halt.

Points out former Seattle superintendent Joseph Olchefske:

> School districts have a staggering array of special interests that revolve around them. Some of these groups are very formal and long-standing: PTAs, ethnic and cultural organizations, neighborhood groups, etc. Others can be created almost overnight. Communities have a tremendous capacity to create informal groups in a very short time to oppose specific policies or approaches being considered by a school board. In many cases, these informal groups will disappear the day after the decision. The antidote to these blockers of change is broad public support for the board's reform agenda. (Personal communication, December 20, 2004)

Reform governance means more than leading the district. It means leading the community. Board leaders and the superintendent must educate the public, starting with business leaders and elected officials and reaching out to nonprofit and religious leaders, civic clubs, parent groups, and every center of influence in the district. These community leaders must understand and embrace the board's core beliefs, commitments, and theory of action; and eventually a majority of the voters must believe that the district is moving in the right direction.

Building civic capacity is a time-consuming and never ending task, but it must be done. No one can do this work as effectively as board members. They spring from the community, represent the community, are networked with the major centers of power, and are ultimately accountable for the performance of the district.

TRANSITION PLANNING

One of life's great truths is that we are all transitional. Superintendents come and go. So do board members. Reform board-superintendent teams can make significant improvements in large urban school districts in 3 years. But deep systemic change and the emergence of a performance culture require a decade or more. Even then, the journey has just begun.

Urban school reform is not the work of one board-superintendent team. It is the work of a succession of gradually changing teams. Managing this succession requires succession planning by the board-superintendent team for the superintendency and the cultivation of outstanding citizens for future board elections. The box at the far right of the framework (see Figure 2.1) represents this work.

Broad public understanding and support of the board's theory of action enables succession planning to become effective succession management. A board-superintendent team that has built civic capacity reaps its reward when the public supports the selection of a new superintendent committed to advancing what is now the city's theory of action and when school board elections are fought on the issue of which candidate will most effectively provide leadership for accelerating the reform trajectory.

THE REFORM GOVERNANCE FRAMEWORK

The Reform Governance Framework, as seen in Figure 2.1, presents the work of the board as a flowchart above the governance/management line because the board's work flows logically from Core Beliefs and Commitments to Transition Planning. Note, however, that flow arrows move from Transition Planning back to Core Beliefs and Commitments.

Reform leadership can originate with business and civic elites or community and parent activists who find and elect board leaders for reform. Or it can originate with a strong reform superintendent who brings a theory of action to a city and builds civic capacity as he or she educates the board. It matters not. What matters is the board's understanding and ownership of the reform agenda and its effective exercise of the powers of governance to advance the agenda.

The Reform Governance Framework does not describe reality. In the life of board members, everything is happening at the same time. Nothing comes first and nothing comes last. In the real world, board members live more often in chaos than in order. One political crisis follows another. There is lack of clarity or consensus on core beliefs. No theory of action consistently guides the development of reform policies. Conventions on major board processes are not agreed upon or are in constant flux. And no one seems to know for certain, or else everyone has a different idea, about the powers and responsibilities of the board.

Notwithstanding messy reality and the limitations of a static, two-dimensional model to describe it, the Reform Governance Framework is a powerful tool to help board members understand their work and guide their actions as reform leaders. The following chapters are an explication of the Reform Governance Framework, supported by examples that place theory in the real world of school board members.

CHAPTER 3

Core Beliefs and Commitments

CORE BELIEFS AND COMMITMENTS are the conceptual starting point for the work of a school board. What do the board members believe about children and their capacity for learning, the purposes of public education, the school effect, and the performance potential of school districts? And what are their commitments?

Board-superintendent teams that request board training frequently want to begin with relationships (particularly the relationship between the board and the superintendent) and the major processes by which the board does its work. This is appropriate. Often, relationships are dysfunctional and processes ineffective. If this is so, consideration of roles and relationships is the place to begin.

The Reform Governance Framework permits analysis to begin anywhere, for the flowchart has no beginning and no end. Because core beliefs and commitments are the fountainhead for action, however, logically they come first. This is why the Core Beliefs box is at the top left of the framework (see Figure 3.1).

THE BIG QUESTION

The first question every board member should ask him- or herself, and the question that opens up the entire Reform Governance Framework, is, Am I satisfied with incremental improvements in the status quo, or am I profoundly dissatisfied with the status quo and determined to change it as quickly as possible? This is the big question. One answer leads to governance primarily as oversight, the other to governance primarily as leadership for change.

Why would a board member be satisfied with only incremental improvement in the status quo? Is there a district anywhere that has all children performing at grade level, all children performing to their potential, and no academic-achievement gap?

Perhaps board members in some suburban districts believe they are so close that they can reach their goals with incremental improvements. Maybe

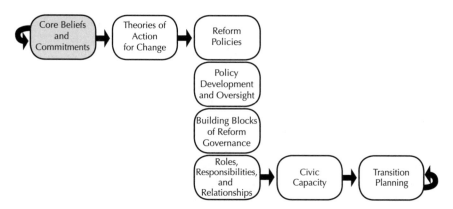

Figure 3.1. Core beliefs as element of Reform Governance Framework.

some can, though with rare exceptions even wealthy suburban districts with mostly middle-class children have significant achievement gaps and too many children performing below potential. Every urban board member in America, however, should be profoundly dissatisfied with the performance of his or her district and determined to change it as quickly as possible. The times demand it.

The civil rights movement has taught Americans that all children deserve equal opportunity; that separate is not equal; and that sorting children by gender, class, and race is immoral. The global information economy has transformed the workplace, making the nation's standard of living dependent on a highly skilled workforce. And by midcentury, half of all of Americans will be people whose primary ancestry is non-European (U.S. Census Bureau, 2004), which means that unless the achievement gap is substantially eliminated, America's workforce will become increasingly less skilled. Given the moral and economic imperative and the risks to our democracy if America is divided into a nation of haves and have-nots, how can any urban board not commit itself to leadership for change?

CORE BELIEFS AND COMMITMENTS

Leadership starts with core beliefs and commitments. Beliefs and commitments go together, for beliefs not tied to commitments are of little value. There is a big difference between, It can be done, and, It will be done. Boards cannot effectively lead change unless they accept responsibility for results. When a school district fails to improve, it is not the district's workforce that fails; it is the board that fails.

Without core beliefs that children can and must learn and school districts can and must become effective and efficient organizations with the capacity to make this happen, boards will not commit themselves to these outcomes. And without commitment to these outcomes, boards will not have the constancy of purpose and strength to overcome the obstacles to reform—for make no mistake, the reform path is not an easy one. Those who benefit from the status quo will fight to maintain it.

Each board must clarify its own core beliefs and commitments. There can be many, though no board can focus on a long list. Certainly the list must include the following: All children can and will learn at high levels; all children will reach their learning potential; the achievement gap can and will be eliminated; the school effect can and must be much larger than it currently is; and school districts can and must become high-performing organizations.

All Children at Grade Level

Job one for every school district is making sure that all children take a solid academic curriculum and perform at grade level through high school. Children without a solid high school diploma—indicating proficiency in English, mathematics, science, history, and technology at a minimum—face a bleak future.

Can grade-level standards be determined? Yes, by tracking backward from what a child must know and be able to do to graduate from high school. Can standards change? They must, as the knowledge base expands and the workplace changes. Can all children perform at grade level? Indeed, some children by birth or accident have severe learning disabilities and cannot. The U.S. Department of Education accepts only 1% in this category (Wenger, Kaye, & LaPlante, 1995; Goldstein, 2004). Even if the number is as high as 5%, the rest—a reasonable definition of *all*—can.

Of course, not all children can earn a doctorate in physics. Not all can become brain surgeons. But all can earn an academic high school diploma. Some will work harder and longer, but the standard is attainable. The experience of many high-performing low-income schools in America and the high performance of some low-income countries support this core belief (Mehrotra, 2000).

All Children to Potential

All children performing at grade level is not enough. Because human ability varies enormously, because some children learn faster than others, because some children can become physicists and brain surgeons, school boards should commit themselves to the goal of all children reaching their learning potential. A child who can perform well above grade level but is not given the opportunity for advanced learning may not be seriously damaged for life, but he or she is not served well and society is the loser for it.

No Achievement Gap

Urban boards must have a third core belief and commitment: The academic-achievement gaps between White and Asian children as compared with African American and Hispanic children can and will be eliminated. This may seem redundant to those who believe that if all children perform to their potential the achievement gap will be eliminated. But it is important to state this core belief and commitment separately. School boards need to understand just what the achievement gap is and how it is measured, and doubters must be acknowledged.

The achievement gap is simply a measure of differences in achievement between students of different racial backgrounds. The achievement gap will be eliminated when the achievement curves of the scale scores of African American and Hispanic students mirror those of White and Asian students. When this happens, not only will the average achievement of compared groups be roughly the same; more important, the distribution of students along achievement curves will also be roughly the same.

This definition is a more challenging definition than the definition of most educators, policy makers, and researchers. Until the 1990s, many studies of the achievement gap focused on group differences between African Americans and their White peers in average achievement on norm-referenced tests. Researchers found that though some African American students performed very well and some White students performed quite poorly, African American students, on average, consistently performed worse than their White peers. Comparisons using norm-referenced tests provided information on how students performed in relation to their peers, but not in relation to agreed-upon levels of proficiency.

During the 1990s, the standards movement pressed states and districts to consider new definitions of achievement and to narrow the achievement gap. First, as many states introduced criterion-referenced tests that measured student achievement relative to learning standards and performance benchmarks, researchers simplified their definitions of achievement by measuring the percentage of students reaching various performance levels set by previously determined cutoff scores on tests. Additionally, educators in some states were required to report performance for major ethnic groups—White, African American, Hispanic, Asian, and Native American—as well as by gender and economic circumstances. NCLB follows this model.

The problem with the NCLB approach is that measuring gaps based on the percentage of students reaching various proficiency levels is inadequate. States can minimize the appearance of achievement gaps by setting a low bar, thus ensuring that more students of different racial groups and income levels are deemed proficient. Some schools and districts have tried to obscure the achievement gap using a different strategy: concentrating attention on moving students just under the bar to just over it, while paying little attention to students who test well below proficiency.

A better way to assess the achievement of student groups is to compare average scale scores of students—that is, rather than comparing how many students of different backgrounds can jump the bar at four feet, compare the average height cleared by African American students to the average cleared by White students. Unfortunately, measuring gaps with average scale scores has problems as well. It is possible that differences in average scores can narrow because a handful of very high achieving students drive up the average achievement of the group overall, while the bulk of students remain below average.

For all these reasons, the best way to understand the achievement gap is to compare not only average scale score achievement on criterion-referenced tests, but also the distribution of achievement within subgroups. This approach recognizes that not all students will be able to achieve at the same level; there will always be ranges of achievement within any group of students. However, it also recognizes that the ranges of achievement should be roughly the same when comparing two groups of students who have access to the same education and that no subgroup of students should be achieving disproportionately below the levels of other subgroups. The theory and mechanics behind this approach are provided by Handcock and Morris (1999).

Using cutoff levels and comparative distribution indicators, school boards can obtain an accurate snapshot of their district's overall achievement gaps. What school boards need to fully comprehend their achievement gaps and identify trends for policy and management action is a series of these snapshots, taken over 3 or 4 years, which could be compared with similar snapshots from districts serving similar students. School boards will also want to understand achievement within their districts by using comparative distributional indicators to analyze performance by grade level and by school, comparing where possible schools that serve similar populations. It is difficult to see how a district can effectively act to eliminate the achievement gap without such information to guide the allocation of personnel and targeted instructional approaches.

Many Americans believe that a situation in which all children perform at least at grade level is a stretch, let alone no achievement gap. These doubters give many reasons: continuing discrimination against people of color, prenatal and early childhood nutrition, the culture of poverty, the culture of race, or even genes. Whatever the reason, these doubters don't believe that the performance curves of African Americans and Hispanics can be elevated to match the performance curves of Whites and Asians.

Indeed, nowhere in America has the achievement gap been eliminated in a large population. The salient fact is that, in general, White and Asian children begin school with an academic edge that persists throughout their years in school. Even when students of different backgrounds begin at the same academic level, students of color appear to slowly fall behind their peers over time (Phillips, Crouse, & Ralph, 1998). By the 12th grade, while 75% of White students and 70% of Asian students demonstrate at least partial mastery of basic reading skills on the NAEP, only 40% of African American students and 44% of Hispanic students do (Donahue, Daane, & Grigg, 2003). In math, the gaps are just as wide (Braswell, Daane, & Grigg, 2003).

Furthermore, racial disparities among the highest- and lowest-performing American students are clear. Among high school students, African Americans are about six times more likely to score in the bottom 5% of the distribution on a composite measure of academic skills compared to Whites. White students, by contrast, are 10–20 times more likely to score in the top 5% (Hedges & Nowell, 1998). The achievement gap is wide and deeply embedded in American culture (Jencks & Phillips, 1998; J. R. Campbell, Hombo, & Mazzeo, 2000; Haycock, Jerald, & Huang, 2001; National Center for Education Statistics, 2001).

There has been progress toward narrowing the achievement gap at moderate performance levels. But nowhere has the full performance curve of African American and Hispanic children matched the performance curve of White and Asian children. To use a high-jump analogy, if the bar is set moderately low and the measure of performance is the percentage of jumpers who clear it, over time the performance gap between subgroups of jumpers will narrow. This is what has happened in states such as Texas that have assessed performance at moderate levels. The achievement gap has narrowed. But if the measure is how high each jumper can jump, the performance gap in Texas remains unchanged.

So on what evidence can urban boards commit themselves to eliminating the achievement gap, that is, merging the performance curves for African American and Hispanic children with those of White and Asian children? Evidence shows that genes most certainly do not explain between-group performance differences, that America has consistently failed to provide adequate educational opportunity to its poor children, that from the mid-1970s to about 1988 the achievement gap in America narrowed, and that culture can provide an achievement advantage or disadvantage. Also, a fair number of schools have demonstrated that low-income and minority students can achieve at high standards and that gaps in achievement can be narrowed (Thernstrom & Thernstrom, 2003; The Education Trust, 2002; Loveless,

2003). Furthermore, there is the argument from the standpoint of logic. Just because something has not been done does not mean it cannot be done. Throughout history, leaders have believed they could do great things that had not been done before, and have done them.

Effective Schools

Doubters of these commitments will point out that the school effect is not 100%; families and societies contribute to or impede learning. This is certainly true. The question, however, is whether the school effect is small or large. If what a child learns is determined solely by what happens outside school rather than by what happens in school, then schools are not important and there is little reason to make them better. But if schools can fundamentally affect what children learn and how well and fast they learn it, then schools matter and improving them is an imperative.

Researchers (Coleman et al., 1966) used to believe that the school effect was small. That is, measured school characteristics predicted very little about differences in student achievement in comparison to other variables like parent education and family income. With improved data and statistical methods, however, many researchers (Teddlie & Reynolds, 2000) now contend that school effects are larger than once believed, particularly with regard to the rate at which students learn.

Among the school factors that researchers say matter, teachers and school climate are central, and the effects of good schools and teachers may be additive. One "value-added" study (Sanders & Rivers, 1996) showed that children who are assigned to three highly effective teachers in a row scored at the 83rd percentile in math at the end of fifth grade, while children assigned to three ineffective teachers in a row scored at the 29th percentile.

In reality, we do not know how large the school effect is, or, more important, how large it could be. But evidence is mounting that schools matter a great deal, in particular for low-income and minority students. Board members who wish to become effective reform leaders must believe that the school effect in their district can be huge and then commit themselves to making it happen.

Commenting on this point, Boston superintendent Payzant asserts:

> It should not be the business of America's schools to predetermine what students can and cannot do. If we've learned anything in the past 2 decades about schooling, it's that innate ability is impossible to assess apart from environment, and that effective teaching and learning can result in very high levels of achievement for all children. (Personal communication, January 3, 2005)

This does not suggest that the effects of family background and societal factors are insignificant. Neither does it mean that schools can do the job alone. Closing the achievement gap will very likely require addressing simultaneously the social, economic, and educational needs of children. Most urban school districts lack the resources, strategies, and desire to do that on their own.

That said, however, someone must lead the charge to close achievement gaps, and school boards are the right organization to do so. No other public body is more directly responsible for the academic achievement of young people, and board members, as the elected or appointed leaders of their district, can bring communities together to make eliminating the achievement gap a core belief and commitment for all.

Effective School Districts

One essential core belief and commitment remains: Urban boards must believe that urban districts can become high-performing organizations. A lot of people don't think they can. Some believe urban districts and the boards that govern them are so hopeless that they should be abolished. Let charter schools and vouchers meet the educational needs of urban children, they say. Indeed many urban districts have been governed and managed poorly. And not many come even close to the performance standards of America's best private companies. But notwithstanding the challenges of public-sector management and urban politics, school districts can become high-performing organizations if board members make this a priority.

Boards must accept no excuse for ineffective and inefficient business operations. Finance and accounting, human resource management, purchasing and inventory management, facility maintenance, food service, transportation, and construction management in school districts are more like than unlike business functions in other organizations. School districts can and should be world class in business operations. A few are approaching this standard in some areas and perform as well as many private-sector companies. Boards must believe that their districts can become high-performing organizations, insist that they do, and give their superintendents the power to make it so.

Boards may have other core beliefs and commitments than the few outlined here. Democracy places many claims on public education. Nevertheless, boards should keep their core beliefs and commitments to a minimum. *Core* means just that—those beliefs and commitments at the center of others. Too many commitments blur focus and lead in practice to no commitments.

The beliefs and commitments put forward here may sound utopian, but sufficient evidence exists to persuade us that with time and the focused use of available resources, all are achievable. Board members who do not share these beliefs and do not make these commitments will not transform urban districts. Those who do might.

Faith in ultimate success drives all successful human enterprises against great odds. Most would agree that the odds against achievement of the preceding commitments are high, but all must agree that the stakes are even higher, that the work must be done, and that those who have the power to do it are the men and women who serve on America's urban school boards.

Ultimate success is not assured, but boards that commit themselves and act on their commitments are guaranteed huge improvements. Board members unwilling to make these commitments and act upon them do not deserve the power placed in their hands by the people who elected or appointed them.

STANDARDS AND ASSESSMENTS

Boards that commit themselves to the core beliefs noted above must commit themselves to standards and assessments. If student achievement is to mean anything more than good intentions, good feelings, and the assurance of teachers that children are learning, there must be content standards, performance standards, assessments, and expectations for improvement. Otherwise one cannot answer the question, Are the children learning?

States have accepted the responsibility, some better than others, of setting content standards (what should children know and be able to do), performance standards (what level of performance is acceptable), and assessing performance (by criterion-referenced tests aligned to the standards). NCLB requires all states that accept federal money for K–12 education to measure student achievement and show annual progress.

Without doubt, standards can be ill chosen and measures of performance unaligned with standards or too narrow to provide comprehensive assessments. Standards-based reforms that are poorly designed or poorly executed, however, are no reason to throw out standards and assessments, as some critics recommend. Board members should use their influence with state policy makers to continually improve state standards and assessments.

In addition, boards can establish district content or performance standards and assess student achievement using measures of performance other than those required by the state. Boards committed to student learning and high performance in all district operations should establish standards and goals for every commitment they make and measure performance. By doing so, they will focus the attention of the public on the work of the district, build public support for their commitments, and motivate the workforce to concentrate on high-priority work. What boards value, they must measure, for what gets measured gets done.

THE HOPE FOR AMERICA

Urban districts are the hope for America. As they go, so will go the nation. They must educate children as effectively and efficiently as the best suburban districts and private schools. That they do not now is not proof that they cannot. Board members must believe that their districts can achieve excellence and commit themselves to this result.

What about charter schools and voucher programs? Are they a better hope? Many say yes; many say no. For both, the evidence of positive impacts on student achievement exists and, in the case of charters, appears to be growing stronger. But the results are not universal.

Critics point out that children in some charter schools do not appear to perform better, on average, than children in public schools; that some charter schools have failed; and that, in any case, charter schools drain money away from public schools. Charter supporters point to growing evidence that charter schools, especially those serving at-risk children, improve performance more quickly than traditional public schools; that many traditional public schools have failed for decades; that public school costs go down as they have fewer children to educate; and that in most cases charter schools receive significantly fewer dollars per child than traditional public schools.

The results from several state and national studies suggest that "overall, there are no conclusive data to indicate that charter schools are on the whole failing their students and some charter schools are showing positive achievement results" (Bulkley & Fisler, 2002, p. 23). Looking at data across 10 states between 2000 and 2002, Loveless (2003) found that while charter students' test scores started lower, on average, than those in traditional public schools, achievement in charter schools improved at a faster rate. However, findings from even the best studies should be viewed with caution, as most have compared average achievement (both levels and gains scores) of children in charter schools with district and state averages rather than with those of children who wanted to attend a charter school but did not obtain a spot (Allen, Cotter, & Marcucio, 2003; Bulkley & Fisler, 2002; Gill, Timpane, Ross, & Brewer, 2001; Goldhaber, 1999; Hassel, 1999; Vanourek, Finn, & Manno, 2000).

There is no end to the debate on charters. Both proponents and opponents, however, agree that accurately measuring the impact of charter schools is complicated, and indeed it may be years before the weight of evidence settles squarely on one side or the other.

The debate on vouchers is even more spirited, with many seeing vouchers as the great hope for America and many others viewing them as the sum of all fears for public education. Proponents argue that vouchers provide students with a needed escape from low-performing public schools and that the competition created by the availability of vouchers will press school districts overall to improve. Critics of voucher proposals argue that they are an illegitimate use of public dollars, especially when applied to attendance at religious schools, that the "creaming" of motivated parents and students from public schools will harm students left behind, and that the true ambition of voucher proponents is to privatize education in the United States.

Studies conducted on voucher programs to date provide information primarily about student achievement and parent satisfaction and less so about the effects on the schools and districts left behind. Research on New York; Milwaukee; Dayton; and Washington, DC, indicate some positive impacts for African American students, especially in the area of math, and high levels of parent satisfaction. Evaluations of several other cities' efforts, however, have produced mixed results (Gill et al., 2001; Hadderman, 2002; Peterson & Campbell, 2001).

Perhaps, in time, research and public opinion will resolve these controversies. In the meantime, one overwhelming fact stands out: The vast majority of America's urban children are in traditional public schools, and that is almost certainly where they will remain. As Susan Wilkinson, former board chair in Duval County, Florida, urges: "Charter schools and vouchers should not threaten school boards. Their focus needs to be solidly on improving their district instead of spending valuable time and energy on this battle" (personal communication, January 4, 2005).

School districts, not charter schools and voucher programs, will educate, or fail to educate, the vast majority of this generation of American children. This is why making them high-performing organizations is the nation's highest domestic priority and why the board members who govern them are in a position to be the nation's most important school reformers.

CHAPTER 4

Theories of Action
for Change

BELIEFS AND COMMITMENTS LEAD to action. But what actions by a board will create a high-performing district? Many boards get stuck on this point. Some go directly from core beliefs and commitments to goals and a strategic plan. This is a mistake. Standing between beliefs and commitments and goals and plans is a theory of action for change (see Figure 4.1). Boards need to and should welcome the assistance of their superintendents in developing a theory of action, but clarifying and explicitly stating one is their responsibility.

THEORY OF ACTION FOR CHANGE

What is a theory of action for change, why must it precede goals and plans, and why is it so important? A theory of change is a set of beliefs about what motivates people and how organizations or societies work. A theory of action is a guide to actions that, given a theory of change, will achieve desired results.

In the school reform context, a theory of change is a set of beliefs that encompasses how children learn, what drives the behavior of the adults, the conditions that create organizational excellence, and the interplay between American democracy and democratic institutions. For a school board, a theory of action is a set of beliefs, given the board's theory of change, about what board actions will lead to the fulfillment of the board's commitments.

For example, does the board believe that people are intrinsically or extrinsically motivated? What does the board believe about the impact of organizational structure? What will change a system that is complex, open, large, and dynamic? Depending on the answers to these and other questions, how should the board act?

James Coleman proposed the theory-of-action approach to social policy in 1986 as an organizing principle to bring together the beliefs and actions of individuals toward a collective goal (Coleman, 1986). Paul T. Hill, more than anyone, introduced theory-of-action thinking to explain urban district reform initiatives (Hill, Campbell, & Harvey, 2000; Hill, Celio, & Harvey, 1998; Resnick & Glennan, 2002).

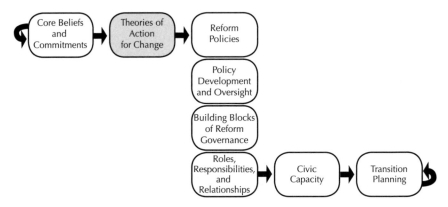

Figure 4.1. Theories of action as element of Reform Governance Framework.

There are many partial theories of action for improving student achievement in urban districts: smaller schools, smaller classes, investment in prekindergarten education, more stringent requirements for entry into the teaching profession, less stringent requirements for entry into the teaching profession, variable pay, merit pay, whole-school designs, school-based management, decentralization, weighted student funding, literacy coaches, public school choice, and so forth. Some people believe that urban districts, as monopoly suppliers, cannot be reformed and that only the marketplace can provide good schools for all children. Their theory of action is charter schools and vouchers.

Boards should not go directly from beliefs and commitments to goals, strategic plans, and policies, for these explicitly or implicitly assume a theory of action. Lack of clarity about the theory of action can lead to unrealistic goals that are based more on hope than analysis, strategic plans that lack coherence, and policy churn. Policy churn, the frequent abandonment of one set of policies for another as new superintendents attempt to put their stamp on a district, or the piling up of new unaligned policies on unimplemented old ones, results in confusion and cynicism in the workforce and low performance (Hess, 1999). Unfortunately, policy churn is common in urban districts precisely because many boards fail to establish a clear theory of action, build public understanding and support for it, and sustain it over the tenure of successive superintendents.

Value Propositions

All successful organizations have an explicit or implicit theory of action: "These (coherent set of) actions on our part will lead to these (some specific, usually quantifiable) results." In the business world, this is called a *value proposition*. An entrepreneur or corporate leadership team posits that a particular business model will attract sufficient customers at a sufficient price to pay costs and leave enough money for a reasonable profit. Sometimes the value proposition is built on price (Wal-Mart), sometimes on quality (Mercedes), sometimes on convenience (Amazon.com), sometimes on customer service (Nordstrom).

Consider the value propositions of two successful companies with innovative business models: Southwest Airlines and Dell. Southwest Airlines recognized that a passenger aircraft only makes money when it is in the air. So to reduce average gate time from more than an hour to 15 minutes, Southwest chose point-to-point flights rather than a hub-and-spoke system, no assigned seats, no meals, and one type of aircraft, among other features. Planes did not need to wait at the gate for multiple connecting flights. Ground crews could service planes quickly, and passengers could turn in their color-coded plastic boarding passes and board quickly. Results: Southwest Airlines sold inexpensive tickets, flew with few empty seats, and became one of the few profitable airlines in the history of commercial aviation.

Michael Dell recognized that computer components had become commodities, that people wanted custom-designed computers, and that the lean production techniques pioneered by Japanese automobile companies could be applied to computers. Dell developed a pull system built on telephone or Internet custom orders and just-in-time production. Results: Dell eliminated inventory and retail distribution costs, gave customers personalized computers for low prices, and made huge amounts of money.

Both the Southwest Airlines and Dell value propositions started with low price as the key to profits. But neither sought low price by following the standard practices in their industry sectors. Rather they developed innovative business models that put together into one package low price, customer satisfaction, high volume, and high profits.

Whole-Systems Change

School boards must approach the challenge of developing effective theories of action with the same thirst for knowledge and creativity that business leaders give to developing value propositions. This means they must be knowledgeable about how the prevailing 20th-century urban district model works, perceptive about the structure and dynamics of large organizations, familiar with the literature on urban school reform in America, and informed about what is being tried and what is working in other urban districts.

Board members with this knowledge will know that urban school districts are complex systems; open to numerous outside influences; large, with all the problems that come with size; and, though fundamentally stable, in constant change. They will know that school improvement requires district improvement; that what affects one part of the system affects numerous other parts; that changes not rooted in an understanding of whole systems frequently have unintended consequences; and that improvement is not doing one thing exceedingly well, it is doing many aligned things well. They will also know that a theory of action for their district must be built on the experience of other high-performing organizations, not only, but certainly including, other urban districts. And they will know that a theory of action that does not take into account politics, and especially the political life of their city, cannot succeed.

Armed with this knowledge, and building on their core beliefs and commitments, urban boards can and should explicitly state their theory of action. It will inform, guide, and keep in alignment goals, plans, policies, and budgets. Boards that go directly to goals and plans and approve policies in a reactive mode—in response to ideologues, the pressures of the day, and specific events—risk, at best, minimal improvements and, at worst, spinning wheels, waste, and chaos.

COMPREHENSIVE THEORIES OF ACTION FOR INCREMENTAL IMPROVEMENTS

One can identify numerous partial theories of action—smaller classes, decentralization, and others, as referenced above—but what boards need is a comprehensive theory of action that provides a policy framework for aligned reform policies, dictates organizational structure, and produces over time a district culture. The starting point for writing a theory of action statement is the Big Question: Are board members satisfied with incremental improvements in the status quo or profoundly dissatisfied with the status quo and determined to change it as quickly as possible?

There are several theories of action that will meet the needs of a board satisfied with incremental improvements in the status quo. These can be grouped under the heading "Fine-Tune the Prevailing System." The premise of these theories is that the prevailing 20th-century system for organizing and managing school districts is the best one and that what is needed to improve student achievement is to make the system work the way it is supposed to. What districts need to do is make certain that all teachers are certified for the grade or classes they teach; that all students have textbooks on the first day of school; and that schools are safe, classrooms orderly, facilities adequate, buses timely, and food healthy and tasty.

What is needed to make all this happen? Two comprehensive theories of action stand out in the national debate about how to improve urban schools: more resources and effective management.

More Resources

More resources, say many, is the most effective means by which to improve achievement. Public schools are underfunded. Teachers are underpaid. School districts need to provide smaller schools, smaller classes, prekindergarten for all children, more technology, better facilities, and social services for at risk children, among other things.

What almost might be called a subset of the more resources theory of action is the focus on programs. Many community activists, politicians, and board members believe that the most effective way to respond to a problem is to create a program. So programs are created for parental involvement, attendance, dropout prevention, tutoring, and after-school instruction; and these are layered on top of routine school management. As the number and size of programs grow, so grows the number of Central Office administrators needed to oversee these programs, and so grows the percentage of district dollars controlled by Central Office staff.

Whether to more adequately fund salaries, facilities, technology, and other routine operations or to expand programs, more resources are the key, say the advocates of this theory of action. To continue funding at current levels harms poor children, perpetuates racism and classism, and is unconscionable.

The more-resources theory of action is widely embraced within the education establishment—by school board associations, administrator associations, teacher unions, colleges of education, and state education officials. It also receives wide support among public school advocates and the political Left. Supporters do not suggest that the 20th-century model fully meets the needs of the 21st century. Prekindergarten, social services, technology infrastructure, and new programs to meet newly identified needs are required. They do suggest that with adequate resources with which to fund these and other needs, school districts as they are now organized and managed can provide what urban children need. The problem is not with the system; it is with those who will not provide adequate resources.

Effective Management

The effective-management theory of action states that improving management is the most effective way in which to improve urban districts. This theory is also based on the premise that the prevailing 20th-century model is the best paradigm for delivering education to children. It asserts, however, that public education does not need more resources; school districts do not make effective use of the money they have. What they need is not more resources but better management.

The effective-management theory is attractive to business leaders; low-tax, small-government advocates; and many on the political Right. Unlike supporters of the more-resources theory, they tend to be critical of the education establishment. But their criticism is not directed at the system as much as it is at the people who manage the system.

Within this theory are two major approaches. The first emphasizes outside expertise. The premise is that school people lack the knowledge and skills necessary to manage large complex organizations and teach effectively. They need help from outside experts: people from business, universities, and not-for-profit organizations. After all, how many superintendents and district administrators have experience in the business world? How many principals have been trained in management? How many teachers have been trained in team building and problem solving or have been provided the necessary professional development to teach to state standards?

What districts need to do is seek and accept advice from business leaders on organizational development, leadership, communication, financial management, procurement, human resources management, facilities management, transportation, food service—in fact, everything that falls under the heading of "Leadership and Management." Meanwhile, universities and not-for-profits can help design and implement board-training programs, superintendent- and principal-preparation programs, and professional development for teachers and in other ways help school people improve their performance. Business groups, many not-for-profit organizations, and numerous foundations support this approach; and urban districts all over America have sought and welcomed assistance and reaped the reward of improved organizational effectiveness.

The second major approach to management improvement is command-and-control leadership. The premise is that the workforce is unfocused, undisciplined, wasteful, and dominated by self-interest. Everyone is doing his or her own thing, some sincerely, some cynically. The organization is broken. What is needed is a strong executive with the power to command behavior and the ability to control it.

The executive, perhaps a nontraditional superintendent, will clean house, replacing burned-out, ineffective Central Office administrators and principals with talented and committed can-do leader/managers, some perhaps with business backgrounds. He or she will bring together blue ribbon committees of external or internal experts to determine best practices for teaching and learning and major business systems, and then through the development of training manuals, training programs, and internal controls, put new systems into place.

Many superintendents and boards believe that command and control is the most effective way to turn around a low-performing district, and command and control is at the root of many of the statutes and rules passed and promulgated by state legislatures and state education agencies. The underlying assumption is that legislatures, boards, superintendents, and others with power can, with the help of experts, determine the best way for things to be done and that strong executive leadership can make it happen.

Outside expertise and command and control are overlapping approaches. Both assume that the 20th-century model is the best system and that effective management will produce the desired results. The focus of outside expertise is knowledge. The focus of command and control is power. Each needs the other. Outside expertise and command and control are different approaches to the same theory of action, namely, the best way to improve urban districts is to improve management.

More resources and effective management as comprehensive theories of action also overlap. They have quite different views about public education, but they share an underling premise: make the system work the way it is supposed to and all children will learn. The more-resources advocates don't seek solutions within the system. They tend to believe that teachers and administrators are doing a great job. The problem is with the politicians and the public, who refuse to provide the necessary resources. The effective-management advocates tend to believe that lack of money is not the problem. Urban districts have enough money to do the job. The problem is with administrators who don't know how to manage and teachers who don't know how to teach.

Again, the difference is one of emphasis. One can believe that urban districts need more resources *and* better management. Most probably need both. Whether a board selects one or the other of these two theories of action, or a combination of both, it is explicitly or implicitly accepting the premise that the prevailing 20th-century model is the best system for organizing schools and school districts. It is affirming that this system, if it is properly funded and managed, can educate all children to high levels and eliminate the achievement gap.

If a board's answer to the Big Question is that incremental improvements in the status quo are acceptable, then selecting a theory of action is simple. More resources or effective management, or the two in combination, will probably do the job. After all, if the district is already delivering excellent results, if incremental improvements are all that are needed to achieve desired goals, then all the district needs to do is keep on doing what it is doing, just do it a little better.

COMPREHENSIVE THEORIES OF ACTION
TO TRANSFORM URBAN DISTRICTS

What about boards, however, that reject incremental improvements—boards profoundly dissatisfied with low student achievement and determined to eliminate the achievement gap at high levels as quickly as possible? Will fine-tuning the prevailing 20th-century model deliver these results? Can a top-down bureaucratic system with one-size-fits-all policies directly operating 100 or more schools, each one organized and managed as schools have been organized and managed for generations, quickly bring all children to grade-level performance and eliminate the achievement gap?

Many Americans think so, as do many state and federal policy makers, board members, and superintendents. At least since the early 1990s, however, there are those who do not. Like the business leaders who created Southwest Airlines, Dell, McDonald's, Federal Express, Wal-Mart, and Amazon.com or the dozens of other innovators of creative business models, these practitioners, researchers, and policy makers have sought a theory of action that goes beyond more resources and effective management. They have been looking for ways to reinvent school districts.

Throughout the 1980s, few education reformers doubted the efficacy of what was commonly viewed as the one best system for organizing school districts. The reformers were business executives and elected state officials, and the reforms coming out of the state legislatures in the post–*A Nation at Risk* period were intended to make the system work better, not change it. Superintendents could do what needed to be done in districts. Boards were not called upon to become reform leaders.

Boards still had important work to do. They needed to provide financial and management oversight, take the lead in campaigns for bond or tax-levy elections, lobby legislatures for additional resources, approve policies required to maintain the smooth operations of the district, and get directly involved in politically charged policy issues such as major facilities construction and renovation, property acquisition, the location of new schools, desegregation litigation, magnet programs, attendance boundaries, school calendars, and textbook selection. This was not unimportant work. And to do it effectively, boards needed all the traditional tools of good governance. But it was not reform leadership.

In the 1990s this began to change. As the standards movement became more firmly established in state policies, and as researchers and practitioners began to think more about systemic change, many eyes began to look more closely at school districts. There was still no consensus on the essential characteristics of high-performing districts, in fact almost no professional literature on districts. But some school boards and superintendents began to question the assumption that fine-tuning the 20th-century model would produce high achievement for all children.

One of these was Joseph Olchefske, then superintendent in Seattle. He said recently:

> As far as we know, Moses did not come down the mountain with an 11th Commandment that described the structure of school districts.

The traditional form of school districts was developed 75 or so years ago by people of that generation for the goals of that era. Clearly, their goals did not focus on high levels of achievement for all students. Our generation has embraced a much more ambitious set of goals spelled out in the standards-based agenda, so it is up to our generation of educators and policy makers to transform school districts to meet the challenge of this "high achievement for all" agenda. (Personal communication, December 20, 2004)

Over the course of the past decade, four comprehensive theories of action for school districts have emerged. All four, it is important to note, build on the foundation of standards-based reform. That is, they require content standards, performance standards, and assessments. Standards-based reform is indeed the unifying theory that brings together all reform theories at all levels—federal, state, district, school, and classroom—for without standards and assessments there is no objective way to know what, if anything, children are learning.

The four theories of action for transforming school districts are performance/empowerment, managed instruction, managed performance/empowerment (a blend of the two), and charter districts. Like more resources and effective management, these theories of action overlap, and they require effective management and benefit from more resources. They are, however, fundamentally different from more resources and effective management as theories of action. They are partial or complete redesigns of school districts.

Performance/Empowerment

This theory of action focuses on results. Student achievement and performance of all district functions are measured in numerous and sophisticated ways, and there are positive and negative consequences for administrators, teachers, and students for meeting performance standards.

Since employees are accountable, they must also be empowered. Participative management and employee involvement prevail, and as much power as possible is pushed out into schools and classrooms. Since students are accountable, parents, on their behalf, are also empowered. They are given public school choice and great influence in the schools they choose. Business leaders usually find this theory of action attractive. Educators often call it accountability and decentralization.[1]

The theory borrows much from quality-management theory and the experience of high-performing private-sector businesses. During the 1980s, Total Quality Management (TQM), building on the work of Edwards Deming and Joseph Juran, on Japanese lean manufacturing, and on the pioneering work of other leading business thinkers, began to transform American business. The focus of TQM, or Continuous Improvement, was on process improvements using statistical tools, data and measurement, participative management, employee involvement, customer satisfaction, and results. Continuous Improvement has contributed significantly to improvements in productivity and quality in American business, including in health care and government services.

The roots of performance/empowerment in school reform reach back to the Kentucky Education Reform Act of 1990, especially to the intellectual leadership of David Hornbeck. Hornbeck was one of the first to see that just as business had to move beyond the factory model in order to produce high-quality products and services in small batches to meet ever changing customer requirements, so school districts had to move beyond the factory model to meet the unique educational needs of communities and individual children. The core idea was to empower those working directly with children to diagnose and teach for results, and by measuring achievement and rewarding results align the interests of teachers and principals with the needs of children. The Kentucky Education Reform Act (1990) was a comprehensive education reform bill stimulated by a school-finance lawsuit, and it included much more than accountability and empowerment, but accountability balanced with empowerment was one of its guiding principles (Foster, 1999; Kentucky Institute for Education Research, 1996; Pankratz & Petrosko, 2002).

In the 1990s, Houston, Philadelphia, Seattle, and Cincinnati embraced variations of performance/empowerment. In Houston, the leadership came first from the board and then, with the selection of one of the board leaders, Rod Paige, as superintendent in early 1994, from superintendent and board. The Houston reformers took their inspiration from the Kentucky Education Reform Act and from the Houston-based American Productivity & Quality Center, which in the late 1980s was deeply involved in the creation of the Malcolm Baldrige National Quality Award.

In Philadelphia the leadership came entirely from David Hornbeck, who in 1994 became superintendent. He came to Philadelphia as "the man with the plan." There is little evidence that the board understood, let alone embraced, Hornbeck's theory of action (Foley, 2001, 2002).

In Seattle, the leadership came from successive superintendents, John Stanford and Joseph Olchefske, and from board leaders. Inspiration came from Edmonton, Alberta, Canada, where Superintendent Mike Strembitsky had used weighted student funding to create the most decentralized urban district in North America. In Cincinnati, Superintendent Steven Adamowski and the board shared leadership (Hawley Miles, 2002a, 2002b).

A close examination of Houston's *Beliefs and Visions* (2001), Hornbeck's *Children Achieving* (1994), what Olchefske called Tight/Loose (2001), and Cincinnati's *Students First* (1996) reveals an underlying belief in the efficacy of accountability aligned with empowerment. Houston, Philadelphia, and

Cincinnati created district accountability systems that rated and ranked schools, attempted to make principals and teachers more accountable for student achievement, and committed themselves to decentralization. Seattle, Cincinnati, and later Houston moved from staffing and program-based school-funding formulas to weighted student funding, with money following the child, and public school choice. All four districts advanced a reform agenda that could be described in broad terms using the definition given above for performance/empowerment, and all four districts produced improvements in student achievement (Foley, 2002; Hawley Miles, 2002a, 2002b; Leschly, 2002; McAdams & Breier, 2003).

One other interesting similarity presents itself. All five superintendents—Paige in Houston, Hornbeck in Philadelphia, Stanford and Olchefske in Seattle, and Adamowski in Cincinnati—were dominating superintendents, and all but Adamowski were nontraditional superintendents.

In recent years, major elements of performance/empowerment are appearing with increasing frequency in large urban districts. In 2003, the Center for Reform of School Systems completed a survey of the nation's 120 largest districts to assess implementation of district accountability systems (McAdams, Wisdom, Glover, & McClellan, 2002). The two key questions for districts were, Does the district rate or rank schools based on student achievement? and Are there consequences? Nine districts met the threshold requirement for having a district accountability system: Atlanta; Boston; Cincinnati; Clark County (Las Vegas), Nevada; Dallas; Houston; Minneapolis; Newark; and San Francisco.

Managed Instruction

This theory of action states that to improve student achievement, districts must directly manage instruction. Many urban children change schools from year to year, even from month to month. It takes 12 to 13 years to educate a child for a high school diploma. Many teachers are inexperienced or lack content mastery. And educators have access to a growing body of knowledge about how children learn and the most effective ways to teach fundamental skills such as reading and math. For these reasons and more, all children in a district must be taught the same comprehensive and aligned curriculum, and all teachers must know how to teach it. Instruction is the district's core business. It must be managed.

Perhaps surprisingly, in the prevailing 20th-century model, school districts manage everything but instruction. Central Office controls staffing, budgets, compensation, schedules, textbooks, procurement—just about everything—and has policies and administrative procedures for almost every conceivable activity. But once teachers close the classroom door, they are left free to do almost whatever they wish. Principals have little knowledge of what goes on in classrooms and assess student achievement by the grades teachers assign. Before the establishment of state standards and assessments, no one could with confidence answer the question, What are the children learning and how well are they learning it? Even with standards and assessments, when one discovers that a child has not learned, it is too late. The school year has ended.

Managed instruction rejects this loose coupling of management with instruction and replaces it with a tightly coupled instructional-management system. Building on content and performance standards, the district constructs a curriculum that covers every subject for every grade in elementary school and every course in middle and high school. The curriculum is coherent, aligned, and detailed down to individual lesson plans, teaching materials, and sample assessments (all of which are available to teachers but not necessarily required).

Professional development is centered on the curriculum and how to teach it, and it is required of all teachers. Curriculum coaches, most frequently reading and math coaches in the elementary schools, provide just-in-time professional development, support teachers in the classroom, and monitor teaching and learning on a daily basis.

Formative assessments are frequent, and a comprehensive student information management system tracks student performance and provides reports to teachers and administrators. Student achievement is disaggregated by classroom, subject, ethnicity, gender, poverty level, and teacher or in any other way that is useful in driving continuous improvement in every part of the instructional-management system. Everything that can be managed is managed.

Establishing and operating an effective instructional-management system is not simply making the current system work better. It is a fundamental change from a loosely to a tightly coupled system. The roles and responsibilities of nearly every adult and nearly every process related to instruction change.

Harvard professor Richard F. Elmore's *Building a New Structure for School Leadership*, published by the Albert Shanker Institute in 2000, analyzes these changes with great insight. It is must reading for every urban school board member. Here is how Elmore describes loose coupling, the standard model for school systems in America in the 1960s and 1970s:

> This view, in brief, posits that the "technical core" of education—detailed decisions about what should be taught at any given time, how it should be taught, what students should be expected to learn at any given time, how they should be grouped within classrooms for purposes of instruction, what they should be required to do to demonstrate their knowledge, and, perhaps most importantly, how their learning should be evaluated—resides in individual classrooms, not in the organization that surrounds them.

Furthermore, the model posited that knowledge at the technical core is weak and uncertain. It cannot be clearly translated into reproducible behaviors, it requires a high degree of individual judgment, and it is not susceptible to reliable external evaluation. Therefore, the loose-coupling argument continues, the administrative superstructure of the organization—principals, board members, and administrators—exists to "buffer" the weak technical core of teaching from outside inspection, interference, or disruption.

Administration in education, then, has come to mean not the management of instruction but the management of the structures and processes around instruction. (pp. 5–6)

Like performance/empowerment, managed instruction appeared in the early 1990s. The pioneering district was New York City Community School District 2, led for 8 years by Anthony Alvarado and then by his former deputy Elaine Fink (Elmore & Burney, 1997a, 1997b).

At about the same time, Superintendent Jerry Anderson was applying similar strategies in Brazosport, Texas. The push came from a board unwilling to tolerate low student achievement, as revealed by the Texas Accountability System, and the original process-management ideas came from the American Productivity & Quality Center, located in Houston (Anderson, 2000). Soon thereafter, Superintendent M. B. Donaldson and his deputy superintendent of curriculum and instruction, Nadine Kajawa, learning from Brazosport, were implementing managed instruction in Aldine, Texas (Henderson, 2000).

Also, at about this time, Pinellas County, Florida, began its journey down a unique quality-improvement path built around the criteria for the Malcolm Baldrige National Quality Award. Again, the spark was provided by the American Productivity & Quality Center, this time with the urging of executives from the school district's local business partner, AT&T Paradyne (Powers, 1998).

By 2000, managed instruction was being implemented to some degree in several large urban districts, among them Boston, Charlotte-Mecklenburg, Duval County, Houston, Long Beach, Norfolk, Garden Grove, Sacramento, and San Diego, and everywhere with positive results (Casserly, 2004; Snipes, Doolittle, & Herlihy, 2002; Supovitz & Taylor, 2003). Three of these districts—Boston, Charlotte-Mecklenburg, and Norfolk—were finalists at least once between 2000 and 2004 for the Broad Prize, which is awarded annually by The Broad Foundation to the urban school districts making the greatest overall improvement in student achievement while reducing achievement gaps across ethnic and income groups. Houston received the prize in 2002, Long Beach in 2003, and Garden Grove in 2004.

In recent years, the Council of the Great City Schools, led by Executive Director Michael Casserly, has become the most powerful force in the nation for promoting managed instruction. Using Strategic Support Teams—experts from other urban districts—the council has provided urban districts with audits of their instructional programs. These audits, which are state-of-the-art descriptions of managed instruction, provide districts with comprehensive road maps for implementation. An increasing number of urban districts are asking for and receiving the benefits of these Strategic Support Teams (Council of the Great City Schools, 2004).

From whence comes managed instruction and how does it fit with performance/empowerment? Managed instruction is in some ways the piece of quality management that performance/empowerment misses. Quality management, remember Deming and Juran, stresses not just data, measurement, participative management, employee involvement, customer satisfaction, and results. At its very heart is the management of process improvement, supported by a range of simple and sophisticated statistical tools. Quality management is all about identifying and managing core processes. Managed instruction is simply applying these process principles to school districts.

Managed Performance/Empowerment

Both performance/empowerment and managed instruction are incomplete as theories of action. Both are comprehensive. Both have been used to excellent effect by urban districts in recent years. In fact, all the urban districts that have made significant improvements in student achievement in recent years—those referenced above and a few others—have adopted one or the other of these two theories of action. But both theories miss something important.

Managed instruction does not create incentives for the adults in the system, does not stimulate innovation, does not build stakeholders, and does not create a performance culture. Rather, by challenging teacher autonomy, it provokes resistance. The phrase used by critics of managed instruction is, *Teachers are deskilled*: They become production workers instead of innovative professionals.

Also, managed instruction tends to reinforce a district's compliance culture. Compliance is the rule for noninstructional processes in the 20th-century model. Now it is also the rule for instruction. Principals and teachers can comply with required behavior but refuse to accept responsibility for results.

Performance/empowerment, with its focus on participative management and employee involvement, solves this problem. By combining accountability for results with empowerment, it aligns adult incentives with student achievement. It creates stakeholders within the organization for the new system, promotes innovation, and gradually transforms a compliance culture into a performance culture.

Performance/empowerment, however, neglects improvement of the numerous major processes that make up the instructional system. It neglects the district's core business. It ignores the huge student-mobility rate in urban districts. And it assumes that principals and their school communities will respond positively to the demands for performance and the freedom of empowerment to produce excellence. Many will; some will not; some perhaps cannot. Performance/empowerment allows too many schools to continue to fail and too many children to be left behind.

How should a district respond to the strengths and weaknesses of these two comprehensive theories of action? A few districts are discovering that a blend of performance/empowerment and managed instruction combines the power and eliminates the defects of both theories of action. When quality thinkers brought together the various principles of quality management in the 1980s, they coined the term *Total Quality Management*. Managed performance/empowerment, perhaps, captures the totality of managed instruction and performance/empowerment. It suggests that performance and empowerment are linked in tight balance, but that empowerment follows performance, and performance is not left to chance: it is managed.

Starting in 2000, the Annenberg Institute for School Reform at Brown University established a School Communities That Work initiative, under the direction of Marla Ucelli, to create a new model for urban districts. Three task forces composed of some of the most creative researchers, policy makers, and practitioners in the nation worked for several years to define and describe a school district that was designed to guarantee equity and excellence for all children. The new design, called a Smart District, is incomplete, but its essential features align closely with what is described here as managed performance/empowerment (School Communities That Work, 2002). Annenberg is now working with several districts to begin implementation of the Smart District design.[2]

Even before the establishment of the School Communities That Work initiative, several urban districts were discovering the power of combining performance/empowerment with managed instruction. Three successful examples are Houston, Boston, and Gwinnett County (Georgia). None of these districts has completely redesigned itself; the work has just begun. But all are on a managed performance/empowerment path. A fourth example, San Diego, illustrates the challenge of moving from the prevailing 20th-century model to managed performance/empowerment.

Houston. Houston started with performance/empowerment in the early 1990s, but began to phase in managed instruction in 1994. This began when Superintendent Paige brought to the attention of the board three important facts: Houston had more than 40 different reading programs in its elementary schools, more than 40% of children transferred from one school to another during the course of the school year, and reading performance was unacceptably low. Soon Central Office was managing instruction in reading, and not long afterward managing instruction in math.

By 2003, Houston had developed online curriculum materials for every subject in every K–8 grade and for all core high school courses, required all teachers to receive professional development aligned with the curriculum, and established a sophisticated student information-management system. Today every teacher has a laptop computer and access through the district Web portal (www.houstonisd.org) to the lesson plans for every class he or she teaches and complete performance data on each one of his or her students. And principals and other district administrators, with proper access codes, can slice and dice student performance data in almost every imaginable way to analyze teaching and learning. This tightly coupled instructional-management system is embedded in a well-developed performance/empowerment system characterized by a sophisticated district accountability system, performance contracts for administrators, promotion standards for students, weighted student funding, and public school choice (McAdams et al., 2002, pp. 39–47).

Boston. Another district with an evolving managed-performance/empowerment system is Boston. The leadership has come almost entirely from Superintendent Payzant, with significant policy leadership assistance from the local education fund, the Boston Plan for Excellence, and with strong support from the appointed board of education.

The name of Boston's program, The Six Essentials of Whole School Improvement, describes the district's instructional system. The six essentials are instructional practice, collaborative school climate, examination of student work and performance data, professional development, shared leadership, and family and community support. The rubrics used to define and measure progress against the six essentials give them specificity and clarity but do not prescribe what schools must do. Schools and teachers are required to create their own professional culture and accept accountability for results. So instruction is tightly coupled, but coupling is a school responsibility, within district guidelines, rather than a district responsibility.

Boston sets student-achievement targets for each school by grade and by race using the Massachusetts Comprehensive Assessment System. The first dimension of accountability is based on academic-achievement data and other quantifiable outcomes, including suspensions and student attendance. Qualitative assessment of the instructional program is added to determine the second dimension of accountability.

A combined school rating describes the school's progress toward specific quantitative goals and implementation of the six essentials. Schools that achieve the highest rating, Effective Practice Schools, receive increased flexibility in their use of professional development resources and are required to share their best practices and expertise with lower-performing schools (Boston Public Schools, 2004; Hawley Miles, 2002c).

Note how the Boston model combines a flexible instructional-management system with performance/empowerment. Instruction is tightly coupled, but coupling is a school responsibility within district guidelines. Accountability is based on instructional processes and multiple outcome measures. And high-performing schools are given increased flexibility.

Superintendent Payzant summarizes the philosophy that supports this system in words that capture the quality management commitment to data-based process improvements to achieve zero defects:

> Our schools can no longer measure their accomplishments just by how the top students are performing. Schools everywhere are now accountable for how all of our students are performing. In Boston, we are relentlessly focused on student performance data throughout the school year to assess progress and to make instructional changes. (Personal communication, January 3, 2005)

Gwinnett County (Georgia). Gwinnett may have the most mature managed-performance/empowerment system in the nation. Starting in the mid-1990s, a resolute and united board, responding to rapid urbanization and public demands for improved student achievement, set out to build a managed-performance/empowerment district. They did not use this label, and their theory of action was not clearly articulated, but they knew what they wanted: district standards, a comprehensive curriculum, professional development aligned with the curriculum, assessments, promotion standards, school and employee accountability, and as much school empowerment as possible within this framework. They also knew that they would not be able to make changes of this magnitude without broad public support, so they committed themselves to maximum community participation in the design of the new system.

For almost a decade, with only minimal turnover, the board has remained true to its vision. Step by step, sometimes amid great public controversy, sometimes in the face of significant employee resistance, sometimes with major delays, but always with extensive community input, the board has put in place a comprehensive managed-performance/empowerment policy frame-work. This achievement is remarkable because Gwinnett, being ahead of its time, could not rely on the state of Georgia for standards, curriculum, and assessments. It had to build its own.

Leading Gwinnett throughout the decade has been Superintendent J. Alvin Wilbanks. He has led the board—while appearing to follow—providing technical expertise, political savvy, and from time to time a shot of courage. Interestingly, he has a strong professional background in quality management (Jenkins, 2004).

San Diego. In Houston, Boston, and Gwinnett, district redesign stimulated controversy. But in San Diego, it divided the city. The conflict there illustrates the challenges of implementing managed instruction and the forces that push managed instruction toward managed performance/empowerment.

Starting in 1998, new superintendent Alan Bersin, a former U.S. attorney, and Anthony Alvarado, hired by Bersin as czar of instruction with the title of chancellor, forced a comprehensive instructional-management system onto a reluctant organization at breakneck speed, angering the teachers union and dividing the city and the board. Bersin survived crisis after crisis with a three-to-two board majority. However, board elections in November 2004 realigned the board, leading to Bersin's early departure in 2005, a year before his contract was to expire. This happened notwithstanding rapidly improving student achievement and a narrowing of the achievement gap in the elementary grades, where managed instruction was most consistently implemented (C. Campbell, 2002; Darling-Hammond et al., 2003; Hess, 2005; Hightower, 2002; Quick et al., 2003).

Bersin and Alvarado implemented managed instruction by command and control. Command and control to fine-tune the prevailing 20th-century model need not create controversy (though management-labor conflict is possible in any workplace if management is inept). When top management requires no significant changes in workforce behavior, there is not likely to be widespread resistance. Bersin and Alvarado, however, were attempting to implement managed instruction in an almost anarchic site-based management system with a powerful, entrenched teachers union.

In 2003, with controversy over managed instruction still at fever pitch, Bersin and some board members began thinking their way through the limitations of managed instruction to a robust managed-performance/empowerment system. Bersin's reflections on implementing managed instruction and his thinking on the need for managed performance/empowerment are captured in the extended quotation below.

> Between 1998 and 2004, San Diego engaged in a significant recentralization of instructional decision making and fiscal management. The purpose was to build coherence into the district, which, in the name of site-based decision making, had fragmented into near anarchy. Each of the district's 180 schools, and most classrooms within most schools, had an instructional program unrelated to what was happening in the next classroom, let alone to classrooms across the district. This fragmentation, atomization, and isolation embodied the lack of a district point of view; it reflected public education's loss of self-confidence. Power relationships and an orientation to process had become the touchstones of legitimacy, replacing student learning and quality teaching as the focus of accountability.

The *Blueprint for Student Success*, our strategic plan for San Diego, was basically a resource-allocation strategy intended to focus resources on aligned instructional methods, professional development, and classroom materials calculated to improve the instructional core. This necessarily entailed considerable political conflict, as existing arrangements were dismantled in favor of focus, frameworks and principal and teacher professional development.

The creation of a focus on student achievement and a strategy for instructional improvement by which to accomplish this reinvented the role of Central Office. It became the center of reform leadership. Our chosen path was excellent leadership at school sites, teacher professional development, modern classrooms and classroom materials, extended learning opportunities for students coordinated with daily instructional programs, and the creation of new relationships between the school and the classroom and between teachers and parents.

Our centralization proceeded also from the premise that managed instruction would produce changes in behaviors that in time would generate among teachers new values, beliefs, and attitudes. After 6 years, gains in student achievement are notable, and it is clear that a large percentage of teachers view instruction differently.

It is also clear that managed instruction is reaching its limits, and that to further accelerate growth San Diego must create virtuous circles of improvement within schools and among individual faculties. Absent this self-generation of continuous improvement, any centralized reform will falter and eventually fade away, unsustained and uninstitutionalized. For this reason, beginning roughly in 2004, "coordinated delegation" is evolving as a critical tool in the change process, both to lock in and to enhance student achievement gains. This is intended to produce over time San Diego's distinctive blend of performance/empowerment and managed instruction.

Having secured quality leadership at school sites and created a coherent political and curricular framework, authority and budgetary power must be returned to school sites. This does not connote a return to fragmentation and isolation, but rather a customization of the reforms to each school site based upon the instructional needs of its students and of the levels of learning of its adults. The instructional core must remain tightly coupled. At the same time, principals, in consultation with faculty leaders and individual teachers, must make decisions about implementation methods and specific "time and money" investments.

Having focused attention on student achievement and developed capacity to accomplish that end, teacher participation in terms of individual growth and faculty collaboration and collegiality must be prime drivers of further progress. The heuristic goal here is to make students the engine of their own learning by teaching them the skills of critical thinking, clear communication, and individual responsibility. Taking the work deep into the classroom and into the marrow of our teachers' practice and students' store of self knowledge can only be accomplished at the school site under the leadership of principals who understand this aim and have mastered their role of implementing continuous improvement.

The work at the school site starts with the development of a school-improvement plan derived from data analyses and designed to improve student achievement by focusing on specific instructional strategies for groups of children or individual children as needed. The work at the system level begins with the design, development, implementation, and oversight of a site-based budgeting system. This will have a dramatic effect both on the schools and on Central Office, which must develop implementation strategies to transform itself into a service organization. The process must be carefully calibrated and introduced over time so that the framework of site leadership authority, consultation, and shared decision making can mature organically. Any effort to mandate this state of affairs and implement it without underlying capacity is destined to fail. The student-weighted funding system, which we have in mind, ultimately will develop a new paradigm for public education in San Diego.

The crucial component here is to develop the appropriate relationship between oversight and implementation. This necessarily raises the issues of tight and loose coupling of various elements affecting the instructional core. One should err, I believe, always on the side of decisions being made closer to where responsibility resides.

The issue of accountability is central: Only with accountability for improvement, measured solely by results reflected in terms of student learning, can this new paradigm retain its integrity and over the long run flourish. The introduction of a district accountability system, as a synthesis of federal and state requirements, is required. Such a system will establish, together with federal law, a framework for responding to high or low performance. The challenge before San Diego is aligning district accountability with the requirements of capacity building. Only when people have been provided with the proper tools and training can they be held accountable for results.

The fulcrum for intervention by the center, in terms of accountability, is the failure of the school to achieve expected results for all of its student subgroups. The extent of both oversight and intervention depends upon levels of achievement. To the extent that all targets are met, there is less oversight and more flexibility.

Key to balancing managed instruction and performance/empowerment is the principal, who serves as the crucial link between the central office and what happens in the classroom. The principal is accountable both to the district and to the school community she serves. The requirement that a principal lead instruction and build a faculty capable of producing quality student achievement is essential regardless of circumstance. The principal is the point at which the school and the district intersect.

The principal similarly is accountable to her school community. No capable leader can proceed without gaining the acceptance of her teachers, parents, and staff. This is the core of legitimacy and a matter of political management, site by site, by the school principal.

The principal's critical role constitutes the antidote both to an overarching central office as well as the weaknesses of site-based management as previously understood. When power is shared in terms of decision making the reference point must be the school relative to the center. The previous understanding that created site-governance teams which voted on matters of curriculum and instruction gives way to this understanding. To the extent that the principal is unable to manage the politics of her site, the center holds her accountable through the process of appointment and removal.

This work defines the objective of a "system" of schools rather than a school system. The emphasis must be upon both the center and the schools, with the role and functions of the center determined by the needs of the schools. In this system the district furnishes a coherent framework and provides principals, working closely with their school community, the delegated authority to organize the school and expend resources consistent with the needs of the children and the need for results. (Personal communication, February 8, 2005)

Metaphors and Comparisons. A useful way to think of urban-district designs is to consider business models. Are schools in a large urban district divisions, franchises, or subsidiaries?

In the 20th-century model they are divisions. Like Toyota assembly plants, all are directly controlled by Central Office, and policies and procedures are fairly uniform throughout the organization. However, for reasons explained by Elmore above, the district's core business, instruction, is not tightly managed. Managed instruction simply adds instruction to what is controlled. Schools, however, are still operated as units in a divisional structure: Central Office rules.

Performance/empowerment is more akin to the franchise model. Franchises can be tightly regulated, like McDonald's, or loosely regulated, like the YMCA. Performance/empowerment is somewhere in between: Central Office "manages the brand" by controlling key business parameters, setting standards, measuring outcomes, and responding positively or negatively to performance.

Managed performance/empowerment is a blend of division and franchise. Some schools are managed directly; others operate more as franchisees, but with varying levels of flexibility depending on performance. And always, Central Office keeps a close eye on instruction, managing it to the level required to meet the needs of the children in the school.

Figure 4.2 shows a way to visualize differences among the prevailing 20th-century model, managed instruction, performance/empowerment, and managed performance/empowerment. The large boxes represent the totality of what goes on in a school: resource allocation, configuration of the workforce, personnel management, schedules, discipline, and so on. The smaller boxes within them represent the core business of every school—instruction—or to be more explicit, curriculum, professional development, teaching, coaching, and student assessment, among other things. The dark shading represents tightly coupled district management, and the white area represents loosely coupled district management.

In the 20th-century model (the top left box), the district maintains tight control of everything but instruction, and employees are accountable for process compliance. In a managed-instruction district (the top right box), the district maintains tight control of everything, including instruction, and accountability remains compliance based. In a performance/empowerment district (the bottom left box), the district continues with a loosely coupled instructional system and in addition gives principals control of personnel, budgets, schedules, and so forth, all this in return for accountability for results.

In a managed-performance/empowerment district (the bottom right box), the district manages instruction with flexibility. That is, it manages more or less of the curriculum more or less tightly, depending on performance and other factors. But schools are given control of almost everything else. Accountability for school management and instruction is performance based, but there are various levels of compliance-based accountability in the instructional area, again based on performance and other factors. In short, the 20th-century model is almost turned inside out: Instruction is now tightly coupled (most of the time) and school management is loosely coupled (most of the time).

Charter Districts

All the highest-performing urban districts in the nation are acting, explicitly or implicitly, on one of the three comprehensive theories of action described

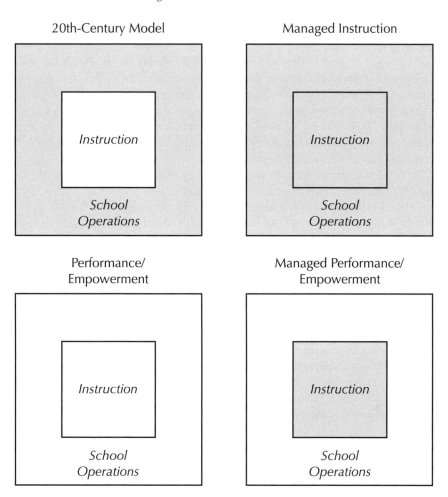

Figure 4.2. District control in various theories of action. Shaded areas indicate tightly coupled district management, with compliance-based accountability. White areas indicate loosely coupled district management, with performance-based accountability.

above—managed instruction, performance/empowerment, or managed-performance/empowerment. A fourth theory of action, charter districts, has not yet been tested in a large urban district. The term *charter district* can have two meanings: a district that operates under a state charter that gives it freedom from state regulations; or a district that does not directly operate schools, but instead grants charters to for-profit or not-for-profit charter operators. This second definition is the one used here.

Of the four comprehensive theories of action considered, charter districts are the most complete break with the 20th-century model. About the only thing they have in common with traditional school districts is responsibility for providing education to children in a specified geographic area. They do this by granting, monitoring, and revoking charters rather than by operating schools. They resemble somewhat the subsidiary-business model: General Electric or AOL Time Warner come to mind, these being parent companies that own and actively oversee, but do not directly manage, different companies, perhaps even companies in different business sectors.

Charter districts were first proposed by Paul T. Hill, director of the Center on Reinventing Public Education at the University of Washington and widely acknowledged as the nation's most creative thinker on the organization and governance of school districts. Hill's idea became the centerpiece of a 1999 report issued by the Education Commission of the States, National Commission on Governing America's Schools, titled *Governing America's Schools: Changing the Rules*. The report describes in considerable detail the operation of charter districts.

At present no major urban district has transformed itself into a charter district, though the Chester Upland District (Pennsylvania), a very small but very urban district in state receivership, contracted out 11 of its 14 schools to for-profit school operators in 2000 (Rotherham, 2001). The Buffalo board approved plans to become a partial charter district, but vigorous opposition from the teachers union helped defeat pro-charter candidates in May 2004 elections, and at the time of writing the plans are on hold. A few large urban districts—Chicago, Houston, Philadelphia, and Los Angeles, for example—have made district charter schools a major part of their reform strategy, but none of these districts has any plans to become a charter district.

The comprehensive theories of action described above do not limit the options available to a reform governance board of education. The redesign of school districts is a new science. We do not know how the innovations described above will play out over time, and we do not know what new models might emerge as districts struggle to find the best ways to educate all children and cope with resistance to change.

One can imagine—indeed the Buffalo board seems to have been moving in this direction—a district that is none of the above. We might call this a *mixed-portfolio district*. Some schools would be managed directly by the district and some would be contracted out to for-profit school management firms or charter operators. Some schools in both categories might be part of, to some degree, the district's instructional-management system, and schools operated by the district would have partial or total freedom in school operations according to circumstances. Finally, expected results, measured by performance level or trend, would vary by school according to circumstances. One can even imagine two charter or mixed-portfolio districts serving the same geographic area and competing for students.

ACCOUNTABILITY, EMPOWERMENT, AND CAPACITY

Whatever theory of action a board chooses, the theory must consider accountability, empowerment, and capacity. These are the three most powerful levers of change available to a board of education, and they are always in play whether a board explicitly uses them or not (Hill et al., 1998).

Accountability is an umbrella word that covers all the forces at work in a district that align the interests of the adults in the system with the interests of children. If there is no alignment other than hope that the adults in the system will figure out what is good for children and organize themselves to provide what children need, high performance is impossible. Not only will the adults be unable to reach consensus on what needs to be done, but there will be insufficient motivation for them to do it.

Accountability means that adults know what results are expected of them, what needs to be done to achieve these results, and what the positive and negative consequences of achieving or not achieving will be. Accountability means content standards, performance standards, assessments, and consequences. Accountability systems have numerous but focused metrics, robust and reliable information-management systems, transparency, personnel-management policies and systems that link job security and compensation to performance, and continuous feedback to drive continuous improvement.

Empowerment means giving the adults in the workplace as much control as possible over how they do their work (but not the freedom to choose their work) and children and parents as much choice as possible about schools, programs, teachers, and so on. Under the umbrella of empowerment are reform ideas such as decentralization, school-based management, weighted student funding, and choice.

Capacity is a measure of the ability of the people and the effectiveness of the systems to deliver on the board's commitments. Do teachers have the knowledge and skills they need? Does the district provide an adequate learning environment and the tools and resources required for teaching and learning? Are business operations effective and efficient?

Accountability, empowerment, and capacity are linked. High accountability requires high empowerment and high capacity. Accountability without matching empowerment creates stress. Empowerment without matching accountability risks chaos. Capacity without matching accountability leads to waste. An effective theory of action recognizes these links and aligns accountability, empowerment, and capacity to achieve the results desired.

Accountability, empowerment, and capacity are the big levers for change. They are the underlying forces in all theories of action. In the majority of urban districts, accountability, empowerment, and capacity are low. Performance metrics are seldom identified, let alone acted upon for continuous improvement. Power resides in Central Office rather than schools. And all too often, facilities are inadequate, major business functions ineffective, and instructional-management systems nonexistent. Principals and teachers, the only people who can educate all children to high levels and eliminate the achievement gap, have insufficient incentive, freedom, and support to do so.

Managed instruction responds to this by building capacity around the district's core business, teaching and learning. Performance/empowerment creates incentives and provides freedom. Managed performance/empowerment balances the imperative to align and manage instruction with the need to respond to the unique needs of school communities, encourage innovation, and create a performance culture. Charter districts rely on the empowerment of parents to choose schools and competition among schools to attract children— in short, marketplace forces—to drive high performance.

As boards come together to develop a clear theory of action, they must be clear about how they intend to balance the use of these three levers to move their district. This work is not easy, and not everyone will welcome it. Accountability, even when balanced with empowerment and capacity, can be threatening.

As Dayton's Littlejohn notes:

> Accountability and empowerment are seldom part of the vocabulary in school districts that are in crisis. Being held accountable even with greater empowerment implies higher standards for performance and consequences if expectations are not met. Quite a few school people, including administrators and board members, would rather not be held accountable for student achievement. And though everyone wants more resources, when capacity building opportunities are provided in the way of professional development, there is frequently resistance. People see and feel the personal risk inherent in the expectations that come with enhanced capacity. It is important that the leaders at the top, including board members and superintendent, be the first to embrace capacity building to correct their own deficiencies and openly accept accountability for results. (Personal communication, February 2, 2005)

CHOOSING A THEORY OF ACTION

Which theory of action should a reform board choose? It depends first and foremost on the board's core beliefs and commitments. If a board is satisfied with incremental improvements in the status quo and does not want fundamental change—and for some suburban boards this may be appropriate— then no theory of action for change is required. Incremental change is the work of management.

A board satisfied with incremental improvement still wants some improvement, still needs to work as an active partner with the superintendent, and must still practice good governance, for there is still much important work to do: hiring and evaluating the superintendent, setting goals, building collaborative relationships, promoting a positive climate, approving policies, overseeing management, and building public support for public education and the district. This is critically important work. But it is governance for oversight and continuous improvement, not governance for reform.

However, a theory of action for change and the board's active involvement in policy leadership is required for boards profoundly dissatisfied with the status quo and committed to rapid and dramatic change. For these boards the question is the following:

> Given everything we know about our situation, the efforts of others
> to improve urban school districts, and the experience of America's
> most effective public or private sector organizations, do we believe
> our district as it is currently organized and managed can be fine-
> tuned to produce the results we must have?

A large number of urban boards have answered this question in the affirmative, not because they have fully understood the structure, processes, and culture of their districts and their options, but because they have not. Many urban boards, fully aware of the achievement-gap crisis and the stakes for America, have assumed that the prevailing 20th-century model for urban school districts is a given; their only option is to fine-tune it. So without other options, they have pushed for more resources and better management, both badly needed. Over time, however, their frustration has increased. Yes, there have been improvements, but fundamentally nothing has changed. Far too many children continue to perform below grade level, and the achievement gap persists.

Other boards, however, have concluded that the prevailing design for school districts, no matter how well funded or managed, can do the job. Redesign is needed. There is no ambiguity where former Seattle superintendent Joseph Olchefske stands on this:

> To me the question of reform or incremental change is ridiculous. All
> you have to do is look at the student-performance data from school
> districts all across America—big and small, urban, suburban and
> rural—to see that school districts as they are currently organized are
> not, and cannot, effectively educate all children to high levels of
> achievement. In fact, I believe school districts have been very well
> organized, maybe even perfectly organized, to ensure that some kids
> would be educated to very high achievement levels while many other

kids would reach only basic skill levels. So, if the fundamental goal of
the standards-based movement is for all students to reach high levels
of achievement, then the only answer to the "reform or incremental
change" question must be an urgent commitment to transformational
change of the current system. (Personal communication, December 20,
2004)

For board leaders who have concluded that transformational change of
the current system is required, there are alternatives. Managed instruction,
performance/empowerment, and managed performance/empowerment have
already shown themselves to be powerful theories of action. Charter districts
are also an option. And there are even more radical ideas circulating: Consider, for example, the impact of overlapping mixed-portfolio districts competing for students in the same geographic area. The decision tree in Figure
4.3 shows the relationship of the theories of action outlined in this chapter
and how they flow from the Big Question.

Choosing and explicitly stating a theory of action is the board's responsibility. This does not mean that the board must create the theory of action;
it can originate with the superintendent or with business and community
leaders. What is crucial is that the board owns the theory of action. A board
that does not understand the theory will be unable to align reform policies
and explain the theory to the public. And a board that is not committed to
the theory will not stand firm when change creates conflict or sustain the
theory when a new superintendent is hired.

However the theory is chosen, the major inputs are the board's core
beliefs about human nature, knowledge about the dynamics of large complex organizations, familiarity with education research, and knowledge about
what is working or not working in other large urban districts. Also, boards
will want to keep in mind the growing power of information technology and
the increasing demand of consumers for choice. And always boards will want
to think deeply about accountability, empowerment, and capacity. The
final input, of course, is local context. All districts are not the same. What
works in one city may not work in another. Table 4.1 illustrates how each
of the theories of action presented might vary along key school and district
functions.

Recognizing the primacy of context, does experience suggest any guidelines for boards choosing a theory of action? Where low performance is
widespread, student mobility is high, a large percentage of teachers are inexperienced or teaching out of field, and teacher turnover is great, managed
instruction should be considered the prime option. This theory of action requires less policy leadership from the board than do the others, for most of
the design work is done below the governance/management line. However,
it does require significant resources for curriculum development, professional

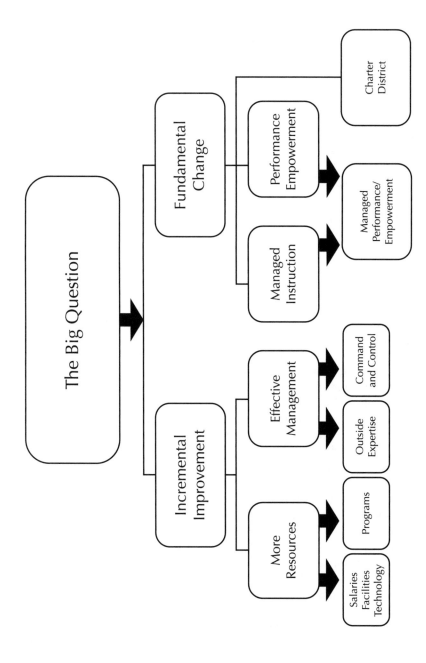

Figure 4.3. Theory of action decision tree.

Table 4.1. Degree of District Control by Theory of Action

	Instructional Management	School Operations Management	School Resource Management	Goals and Performance Measures	Accountability Measures
Managed instruction	Tight	Tight	Tight	Tight	Tight
Performance/ empowerment	Loose	Loose	Loose	Tight	Tight
Managed performance/ empowerment	Varies by school	Loose	Loose	Tight	Tight
Charter district	Autonomous	Autonomous	Autonomous	Varies by school	Varies by school
Mixed portfolio	Varies by school	Varies by school	Varies by school	Varies by school	Tight

development, and a student information-management system; and it requires strong instructional leadership from the superintendent or senior administrators empowered by the superintendent and great sensitivity to the needs of teachers.

Performance/empowerment is a good fit for districts with a strong principal core, a stable core of highly qualified teachers, reasonably effective business systems, and some experience with public school choice, for example, magnet schools. This theory of action requires extensive policy leadership from the board, major changes in business infrastructure, and significant public engagement. Parents and community leaders may not need to know a great deal about managed instruction, but they do need to understand district accountability systems, weighted student funding, and public school choice. Teachers, at least at first, will not likely consider performance/empowerment much of a change, but as school accountability expands to include teacher accountability and as principals assume more personnel-management responsibilities, teachers will be profoundly affected. Principals will see their jobs transformed. Boards must be willing to make an immediate and significant investment in principal development.

For most districts, managed performance/empowerment would not be the place to start. Rather, it would be a transition from managed instruction as more and more district schools reach high performance levels (Boston and San Diego) or a transition from performance/empowerment to meet the challenges of persistently low-performing schools and high student mobility (Houston). However, as Gwinnett County, Georgia, demonstrates, it is possible for a district to start with a managed performance/empowerment theory of action. Note, however, that in the early 1990s Gwinnett was an edge-city district with a stable and experienced workforce, serving a predominately middle-class community and just beginning to feel the effects of urbanization.

Since no large urban districts have yet become charter districts or mixed-portfolio districts, it is difficult to make even preliminary judgments about context and transition issues. In Buffalo, competition from charter schools and an intransigent teachers union made attractive a partial charter district. Most likely, mixed-portfolio districts, if and when they appear, will evolve from one of the preceding theories of action. Two things are certain—it will take significant board leadership and broad public support to create charter or mixed-portfolio districts, and transition issues will be difficult.

Whatever theory of action a board chooses, it must recognize that it is choosing a theory, not selecting a blueprint for district redesign. A theory of action is a guide to action; it has a center of gravity; but it recognizes that urban districts are complex, open, large, and dynamic (COLD) and that management must design and implement within this messy reality. Also, a board must recognize that theories of action can and must be modified over time based on changing circumstances, experience, and research.

But though theories of action evolve, they cannot be junked and replaced every time a new board majority is elected or a new superintendent is hired. District accountability systems, formative and summative student assessments, employee-evaluation systems, variable and performance pay for teachers, weighted student funding, magnet schools, public school choice, full-day prekindergarten for all children, comprehensive curriculum materials, professional development systems, literacy coaches, student information-management systems, outsourcing contracts, district charters, and so on, all driven by a theory of action, commit a district for decades rather than years.

It is because core beliefs and commitments and a powerful theory of action are required in order to drive goals, strategy, and policy that boards of education must be the leaders of urban school reform. Superintendents are the only people who can manage change, and they may even be the primary architects of a district's core beliefs and theory of action, but they cannot commit a community for decades into the future. A board can. Decisions at this level are governance, not management, decisions.

CHAPTER 5

Roles, Responsibilities, and Relationships

SPRINGING DIRECTLY FROM A THEORY OF ACTION are goals, strategic plans, policies, operating plans, and budgets. The first three of these are primary responsibilities of the board of education. That is why in the Reform Governance Framework, the Theories of Action box flows directly into the Reform Policies box, which also includes goals, plans, and budgets.

Note, however, that the Reform Policies box also sits atop a stack of three other boxes labeled Policy Development and Oversight; Building Blocks of Reform Governance; and Roles, Responsibilities, and Relationships (Figure 5.1). The foundation for reform governance is clarity on and commitment to roles, responsibilities, and positive relationships among board members, the superintendent, and community leaders. If board members don't know their job and can't get along with one another, the superintendent, or the major centers of power in their community, reform is impossible. This chapter examines these pivotal roles, responsibilities, and relationships.

THE GOVERNANCE CHALLENGE

Governance is a challenge in all organizations and sectors. As Peter Drucker said of corporate boards in 1974, "There is one thing all boards have in common, regardless of their legal position. *They do not function*" (p. 628). Watching corporate boards in recent years, one is inclined to say that not much has changed.

It is not just corporate boards, however, that frequently don't work. Not-for-profit boards, church boards, school boards, and others frequently don't work. Because governance represents ownership and ownership is usually widely shared, governing boards tend to be diverse and hold many conflicting opinions on important issues. And because the line between governance and management is blurred and sometimes moves, the relationship between boards and chief executive officers is often problematic.

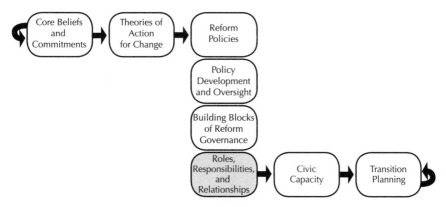

Figure 5.1. Roles, responsibilities, and relationships as element of Reform Governance Framework.

Of all boards that serve the public and private sector in America, few are more challenging than urban school boards. These boards are political: They operate in the public arena under direct democratic control. They deal with extraordinarily high stakes issues: children, community values, and lots of taxpayer money. They have significant responsibility but limited power: They operate as parts of state systems of education. They must govern even though the public purpose of schools lacks consensus and priorities shift over time. The public wants schools to prepare children for democracy, prepare them for the world of work, give them a broad general education, and stimulate their creativity. And more often than not, school board members are not certain what they are supposed to do—reflect or shape public opinion, micromanage, or act as a rubber stamp.

There is no model for urban school boards. They are like but also unlike corporate boards, legislative bodies, and almost all other governing boards. Their roles, responsibilities, and relationships are unique. Like legislative bodies, school boards legislate, but unlike legislative bodies, which coexist as independent branches of government with executive and judicial branches, school boards oversee executive functions and have some judicial functions. Like corporate boards they have fiduciary responsibility and oversee management, but unlike corporate boards they are (as a rule) elected officials and operate in the center of the political arena under intense media scrutiny. And they govern organizations that are critical to the future of America—most of which are low performing. Few university regents, few not-for-profit board members, few members of any governing board, face challenges as daunting as those faced by the board members of America's great urban school districts.

RELATIONSHIP SPHERES

Board members must manage numerous complex relationships: with one another, the superintendent, district employees, union leaders, parents, constituents, business and civic leaders, other elected officials (mayors, city council members, state legislators), journalists, vendors, and others. These relationships can be very complicated, and if any of them sour, effective leadership is compromised.

Board Members

Boards are bodies corporate. Individual board members may have great influence, but legally, boards act as a body and only as a body. Votes count, and if for no other reason than this, board relationships are important. At least a majority of the board must be able to work together. Supermajorities working together are even better.

Board members who want to be effective must treat their colleagues with respect, never fight in public, keep confidences, relate honestly, and in all the other ways that characterize positive relationships get along. Failure to maintain positive relationships with colleagues, even in the midst of serious disagreements and even with colleagues who are self-serving, dishonest, and offensive, makes reform governance difficult.

Maintaining positive relationships among board members is difficult, and throughout urban America, discord among board members is common. This is not surprising. School boards reflect the diversity of America's great cities. Unlike suburban boards, where board members are likely to share common backgrounds, values, and lifestyles, urban board members are likely to be divided by race, class, and ideology. They are more likely to represent single-member districts and the interests of these districts. They must cope with insufficient resources, decaying facilities, high teacher turnover, high student mobility, unsafe communities, and low performance. And they must do all this in the middle of a political arena in which minorities have long-standing and legitimate reasons to mistrust those with power, numerous voices contend to define the purpose of schools, power elites demand immediate improvement of student achievement (at the lowest possible cost), and big-city media put every issue under a magnifying glass. Add to this the fact that most people who seek elective office have strong egos!

There is a double standard. The public expects to see legislatures and city councils deeply divided and engaged in open political warfare. This is unacceptable for school boards. They are expected to work together in harmony for the sake of the children. Unfair, perhaps, but there is a reason for this double standard. The public understands that nothing is more important than children and that a squabbling school board undermines district performance.

Harmony may be unrealistic, but effective teamwork is not. Although most urban boards have one or two board members who are a challenge for their colleagues, it is reasonable to expect a majority, fully reflecting the diversity of the city, to unite behind a common vision and work together as an effective governance team. To my knowledge, this has happened in every urban district that has significantly improved performance, including all those mentioned in this book.

How has it happened? A core group of board members have recognized that diverse viewpoints enhance decision making and even angry colleagues wrong on the facts might be illuminating an underlying point that deserves consideration. They have committed themselves to keeping down the rhetoric, refrained from imputing motives to others, and understood the importance of keeping issues separate, refusing to link support of one issue to support of another and never allowing feelings about a colleague to influence a vote. And they have determined that they will always treat colleagues with courtesy and respect, even when colleagues seem to be asking for just the opposite.

Most important—and perhaps this is the root cause of teamwork—there has been strong leadership on the board. Two or three strong leaders, working together—sometimes even one strong leader—can transform a directionless or even dysfunctional board into an effective board team. Leaders bring out the best in others. In the main, the men and women serving on urban boards are good people, successful in their individual lives even when they are only marginally functional as a collective body. Frequently, all they need for effective teamwork is strong leadership.

Often the board president (or chair) is one of the board's natural leaders, but not always. Some boards rotate the presidency, placing less competent members in the chair from time to time. This makes board leadership more difficult for the board's natural leaders, but it is not an insurmountable barrier. They still lead.

Notwithstanding the desire to be fair or the advantages of avoiding divisive votes over who should be board president, boards are wise to elect as president one of their natural leaders, for the board presidency is important. The president must take responsibility for building positive relationships among board members, keeping the board focused on a few major issues, building consensus, and solving governance problems. Especially, the president must work to maintain positive relationships between the superintendent and board members and assist the superintendent in reining in board members who cross the line into management.

"Mistrust can occur when a board member gossips about board members to other board members or to the superintendent," says San Antonio's Treviño. "Effective board presidents try to keep gossip to a minimum. However, the superintendent and the board president must keep each other aware of misbehaving board members and work together to keep micromanagement under control. These conversations are not gossip, but necessary work" (personal communication, December 24, 2004).

How is this done? If possible, one on one: superintendent and board member, or board president and board member. Sometimes both the superintendent and the board member need to meet with a misbehaving board member, and sometimes issues need to be discussed in an executive session of the board or even acted upon by resolution in an open board meeting. This is not pleasant work, and board members unwilling to do this work should not seek the board presidency.

Board presidents do not need to dominate policy leadership or hog the limelight. Policy leadership on the board should come from those with the interest and knowledge to provide it. And though board presidents are normally the spokespeople for their boards, they are wise to eschew the limelight. Let the superintendent or district spokesperson speak for the district, and when the board needs to speak as a body, create (if possible) an opportunity for the community to see the board acting and speaking corporately. Positive intraboard relationships are the starting point for effective governance.

Union Leaders, Journalists, Vendors, and Parents

For board members, all relationships are important. Anyone with power or influence matters: business and civic leaders, mayors, city council members, state legislators, nonprofit executives, newspaper editorial board members, and so on. Board members should become acquainted with these leaders and become friends with as many as possible. These people are valuable allies when a tax levy is needed or when a crisis strikes. And over time they need to understand and support the board's core beliefs and theory of action. These relationships are the key to building civic capacity (the subject of Chapter 9).

Relationships with union leaders, journalists, vendors, and parents pose special challenges and deserve special attention.

Union Leaders. Union leaders are usually smart, informed, and at the nexus of a great web of power. They share many interests with the board and thus can be great allies, but board members must keep in mind that union leaders do not share their agenda. Union leaders represent the interests of teachers, which are not always the same as the interests of the district.

Keeping on good terms with union leaders is worth considerable effort, and board members should seek opportunities to listen to what they have to say. Union leaders reflect an important point of view, and they have enormous knowledge of what is going on in schools. Board members, however, need to be careful of what they say to union leaders. Although boards have the final say on contracts, managing labor relations is management's responsibility, and it is one of the most difficult tasks in urban education. Superintendents have enough challenges as it is without having board members establishing independent channels of communication with union leaders.

It is best to leave management-labor conversations to the superintendent and his or her staff, especially on contract issues or when contract negotiations are under way. Boards or board members who take it upon themselves to "mediate" relationships between management and labor risk undermining the professionals whom the district has hired to manage these relationships and, in doing so, risk undermining the district. Savvy union leaders are masters at playing the board and superintendent against each other.

Journalists. Relationships with journalists are also challenging. Journalists and board members need each other. Board members help journalists to do their work, that is, to provide comprehensive coverage of the district, and the press is an essential link between elected officials and the citizens they represent. In a democracy, elected officials are accountable to the public and should never refuse an interview; indeed, they should welcome interviews as an opportunity to shape public opinion. However, board members should be careful about what they say.

A free press is essential for democracy to flourish, and most journalists strive for accuracy and balance. They work, however, for newspapers and television stations that are for-profit companies. Mass media companies make money by selling advertising space or time. Their news departments help attract readers or viewers, the basis for advertising rates, by providing information. And controversy spices up the news: "If it bleeds, it leads" is not simply a joke.

Urban districts provide much fodder for the press. Critics complain endlessly; controversy is frequent; unfortunately, bad things sometimes happen in schools; and from time to time there is a financial, personnel, or student-discipline scandal. Reporting all this, even hyping it during sweeps months, when television stations are measuring market share, makes sense for the media.

It does not make sense for board members to help keep these issues before the public. Board members should be trying to build up their districts, not tearing them down. How then can they balance their obligation to be accessible and honest with the media and their need to work through the media to educate the public about their districts and at the same time not play the media's game of hyping controversy?

Here are a few guidelines. Board members should never seek the limelight to promote themselves, always respond promptly to media inquiries, and always tell the truth. However, board members need not answer every question. It is reasonable to engage in a discourse on personal philosophy or national or state issues, explain reasons for votes, or comment on district goals and major policy issues before the board. It is inappropriate to comment on management issues, ongoing scandals or controversies, and unfortunate events that happen in schools. Board members, after all, do not have all the facts on these issues. (And of course it is unethical to share with anyone information on personnel, real estate, legal, or other issues discussed in executive sessions of the board.)

Wise board members, knowing that reporters are skilled professionals and sometimes have their own agenda and knowing that they are not trained in media relations, refer as many questions as possible to the district's communications officer or the board president. The reality is that reporters seldom call except when there is a hot, complex issue, and these are the very issues that are best left to professionals trained to speak for the district or to the board president, who is authorized to speak for the board. "I would rather not comment on that question. You should direct it to the superintendent or the board president," is an honest, and frequently the best, answer.

Vendors. Districts need good relationships with vendors. They supply all sorts of valuable products and services without which high performance would be impossible. Many vendors approach board members when they are pushing a contract, and most want to keep on good terms with board members. After all, boards vote on contracts.

Board members should become knowledgeable about the major vendors that supply school districts with goods and services. Knowledge makes possible penetrating questions when contracts are recommended and supports good board decision making. Also, it is inevitable that board members will become acquainted with major vendor representatives. Board members, however, must manage these relationships with great care.

Selecting vendors is a management decision. One of the most common complaints against urban boards is that some board members promote, even intensively push, contracts with favored vendors. This must not happen. Board members have a fiduciary responsibility to ensure that district contracts are awarded to vendors that provide the best value. Only management has the capacity to do this.

Boards have a management-oversight responsibility to assure themselves and the public that management makes these decisions in the best interests of the district. Management systems are not always effective, and administrators as well as board members are subject to the temptations of friendship, group interest, and favors. As explained later in this chapter, there is a relatively simple way for boards to assure themselves and the public that effective management systems with internal checks and balances are in place.

Having done this, board members should stay out of the vendor-selection process unless asked to participate by the superintendent. (He or she may schedule a board workshop on a major vendor-selection issue, for example, an outsourcing contract.) The board's turn comes when the superintendent has a formal recommendation.

Meanwhile, to avoid a conflict of interest, or even the appearance of one, it is wise for board members to keep vendors at arm's length. Board members should refer vendors to management for official conversations, never make promises, never take favors, avoid any appearance of a special relationship, and most definitely make no attempt to push contracts on the district.

Parents. Of course, parents and constituents are important. Elected board members need no encouragement to be accessible, friendly, and responsive to legitimate concerns. Appointed board members need to be reminded to do the same. The public owns public schools, and one of the primary responsibilities of board members is to build a strong bond between the public and its schools. Parent-Teacher Organization (PTO) meetings, graduations, holiday programs, and award luncheons for volunteers are important events.

Accessible, friendly, and responsive board members, however, do not attempt to obtain favors from the district or solve constituent problems. The difference between constituent service and micromanagement on behalf of constituents is covered below.

Superintendent

All relationships are important, but no relationship is more important than the one between board and superintendent. This relationship can be problematic. For one thing, there are multiple relationships: relationships between individual board members and the superintendent and the institutional relationship between the superintendent and the board. And not infrequently, board members and superintendents have big egos.

The starting point for board-superintendent relationships, states former Duval County board president Susan Wilkinson, is for "both board members and superintendents to put their strong egos aside. It isn't about the board; it isn't about the superintendent; it is about all of the district's students" (personal communication, January 4, 2005).

The biggest problem, however, is that board members frequently, and superintendents sometimes, lack clarity about their roles. Given the difficulty of both jobs and the political context in which the work is done, it is not surprising that confusion abounds.

Both board member and superintendent benefit by understanding the complexity of the other's work. Board members overwhelmed by their own work should keep in mind what superintendents have to do. The latter must manage a large, complex, and highly regulated organization; deliver high performance with limited resources in the center of the political arena; negotiate with multiple unions; listen to parents, business leaders, and everyone else who has an opinion about how schools can be improved; deal with special interest groups who have strong opinions about what is best for children; keep diverse communities happy; and, of course, keep board members happy.

Managing relationships with board members is in fact one of the superintendent's most difficult tasks. When superintendents meet with their peers and no board members are in the room, they talk more about managing difficult boards and board members than about almost anything else. Effective superintendents work hard to understand individual board members and the dynamics of their board. They have a strong incentive to get along; they work for the board.

Everyone has an incentive to get along, but boards, because they are in the position of power, must take the leadership in building solid working relationships. Board members committed to positive, productive relationships with their superintendents will find most superintendents enthusiastic partners.

No superintendent is perfect, but whatever imperfections a superintendent may have, it is the responsibility of board members to do everything within their power to make the superintendent successful. Board members should publicly praise and privately encourage, and when criticism is needed, provide it in the most discreet and positive terms.

At the root of the relationship is trust. Board members must never give their superintendent reason to distrust them, and at the first sign that their superintendent is not deserving of their trust, board members should, again discreetly and in the most positive terms, put the issue on the table and work to resolve it. Disagreement, even spirited disagreement, is inevitable, but maintaining trust is a sacred duty.

San Antonio board president Julian Treviño states:

> It is difficult to hide lack of trust between board and superintendent. District leadership is amazingly transparent, and there are many critics looking to exploit the slightest crack in this relationship. Once trust is undermined, the superintendent's power within and without the organization is weakened, and so is the board's. All the spin-offs are bad. (Personal communication, December 24, 2004)

Board members and superintendents are commonly told by board trainers that it is inappropriate for one board member to have more access to the superintendent than another and that what one board member knows all must know. After all, all board members are equal, and the superintendent works for the entire board, not just for some board members.

This is an ideal, and would that it were possible. But the reality is that, notwithstanding their legal position, not all board members are equal in value to the superintendent or the district. Not infrequently, superintendents develop great respect for the experience and wisdom of individual board members and call on them for confidential advice regarding district strategy, crisis management, or personal or management issues. They may even rely on a strong board member to keep other board members "in line." In many districts, an experienced board member has provided the advice, support, or political muscle that has enabled the superintendent to get through a difficult challenge.

This is appropriate, sometimes even necessary, and no problem if the board member is the board president, but otherwise there are risks. Other board members may come to resent an inner-circle board member. And a superintendent who relies too much on one or two board members—even if they are the ranking board officers—may find him- or herself vulnerable if these board members unexpectedly depart the board.

Also, board members who become advisors must remember that no matter how close the friendship, the superintendent is free to accept or reject advice. Advice offered when none is requested may be perceived as a directive, and no board member, whatever the circumstances, can give a superintendent a directive. Only by formal action can the board do that, and even the full board has no authority to give management directives. Boards govern; superintendents manage.

Here we touch on the core issue in the board-superintendent relationship. Much of the conflict between boards and superintendents arises because one or the other doesn't understand the difference between governance and management. Although there are numerous opportunities for confusion about the governance/management issue, there are five major areas that account for 99% of the confusion. They are core beliefs and theory of action for change, constituent service, management oversight, board meetings, and policy development.

Core beliefs and commitments and theory of action have already been considered. Just to repeat, it is the board's responsibility to clarify and clearly state its core beliefs and commitments and theory of action. Indeed, most boards will want a superintendent to assist them, even guide them, through the process, but it is the board's responsibility to carry out this task. And once the resulting documents exist, though they can be modified over time on the basis of experience and research, they must be modified with care and live on from one superintendent to the next.

In Chapter 6, I examine board meetings, one of the major processes by which the board does its work. In Chapter 7, I delve deeply into policy development. In both chapters, the board's role is clearly outlined. Constituent service and management oversight are the major governance/management issues for the present chapter. They fall clearly under the heading of *roles, responsibilities, and relationships*. But note that they are also process issues.

In fact, all the major areas of governance/management confusion are both role and process issues. Indeed, every chapter in this book is about board/

superintendent roles, responsibilities, and relationships. In the real world what one does and how one does it are inseparable. Remember, the Reform Governance Framework does not describe reality. It is a tool for understanding reality and for guiding action.

Constituent service and management oversight are the two areas where boards and superintendents most often clash. The drumbeat of criticism about urban boards centers on this point: Boards meddle in management. Unfortunately, much of the criticism is deserved. Boards, especially urban boards, have great difficulty keeping above the governance-management line. In short, they micromanage.

Micromanagement comes in two flavors, micromanagement by individual board members and micromanagement by the full board. The first is the most annoying, the second the most dangerous. The root cause of both is politics.

CONSTITUENT SERVICE VERSUS MICROMANAGEMENT

What is the difference between constituent service and micromanagement? Constituent service is helping constituents—in the right way—receive the service the system is supposed to provide. Micromanagement is helping constituents—in the wrong way—receive the service the system is supposed to provide, or attempting to make the system do what it is not supposed to do.

Board members must provide constituent service. All elected officials do so, and appointed board members no less than elected board members must intervene when constituents are not given the service that policy requires. Whether the complaint is broken windows, unsafe playground equipment, late buses, unavailable textbooks, crowded classes, out-of-control classrooms, or absent teachers, board members cannot ignore constituents.

But there is a right way and a wrong way to serve constituents. The wrong way, what former San Diego board president Ron Ottinger describes board members doing in San Diego before Alan Bersin was appointed superintendent, is not infrequently standard practice in urban districts:

> Board members in San Diego had become alternate superintendents under the previous administration. Some submitted hundreds of requests for information or directives to fix issues at particular schools. Chasing these requests ate up significant management time, diffusing and sapping energy that the superintendent, his chief of staff, other top district leaders, and midlevel managers needed to concentrate on management and new reform policies.
>
> In addition, board members attempted to dictate principal selections and barked commands to midlevel staff. District culture

was so dysfunctional that it became normal for principals to bypass the superintendent and go directly to board members if they did not get their way with the administration. This anarchy severely undermined a well-intentioned superintendent who was attempting to focus the system on student outcomes and reading and math instruction.

This changed when Alan Bersin became superintendent. From day one, he struck a bargain with the school board to stop these anarchic practices. Board members agreed to focus on ensuring the effectiveness of management systems and processes, not solving problems, and committed to flow all information through Bersin's chief of staff. (Personal communication, December 21, 2004)

The right way, as Ottinger's quote suggests, is for board members to focus on management systems; follow predetermined protocols to help constituents solve their own problems; or, if this fails, bring problems to the attention of the superintendent or his or her designee. Boards should invest the time required to work with the superintendent in order to develop written protocols to do this work and then stick to them.

With rare exceptions, the first response to a constituent complaint should be to refer the complainant to the appropriate district official, frequently a school principal, and to higher levels of authority if this has already been tried and failed. Principals and other district administrators deserve and appreciate the opportunity to solve problems without having their supervisor bring the problem to their attention. Much of the time, all an administrator needs to solve a problem is awareness that the problem exists.

If a constituent has been rebuffed by the system and the board member determines that, most likely, the constituent has a valid complaint (experienced board members know that some complaints are specious and some complainants are cranks and best ignored), then the board member must become involved. Nonresponsiveness is unfair to the constituent and a disservice to the district.

Some superintendents, especially in smaller districts, want complaints to be brought directly to them. Some superintendents prefer that complaints be brought to the staff of the board services office and then channeled to a designated ombudsperson, perhaps the superintendent's chief of staff, or, if urgent, brought directly to the ombudsperson. Once in the hands of management, the superintendent's designee manages the process on behalf of the superintendent, provides the board member with a report on the disposition of the issue, and provides the superintendent with periodic analyses of complaint patterns for the purpose of systems improvement.

Superintendents are no less keen than board members that districts provide high-quality services to parents and constituents. They cannot know everything. Board members are out and about in the community. They are additional eyes and ears for the superintendent. By bringing unresolved complaints to the superintendent, they not only serve constituents, but also enable management to identify patterns of failure and make systems changes.

This is why protocols for constituent service should require documentation of all complaints that are referred to the superintendent and their resolution. Board members want to know that constituents have received an answer, even if it is not the answer the constituent wanted. Superintendents want to solve problems and improve systems.

Three principles underlie constituent-service protocols: Complaints should only enter the system after front-line managers have failed to solve problems to the satisfaction of complainants, the system must be comprehensive and documented, and board members must never become problem solvers. This last principle is the one that keeps board members above the line that separates governance from management.

No matter how obvious the solution may be; no matter the board member's desire to be helpful; no matter the importance of the constituent—close friend, neighborhood activist, campaign volunteer, or state legislator—board members must not assume the constituent is right or suggest a solution to any district employee, including the superintendent. A suggested solution from a board member can be heard as a directive, and suddenly the board member is making a management decision. Board members must listen to complaints, recommend direct conversations between complainants and front-line managers, or refer complaints to the superintendent following established protocols. That's it.

Trying to solve problems is probably the most common mistake made by board members. However positive the intentions, however beneficial in the short term, the long-term consequences are profoundly negative. Micromanagement sows confusion among district employees, disrupts management systems, and weakens the superintendent's control of the district. By so doing, it diminishes the power of the board to govern. A weak superintendent cannot effectively implement the board's policies or be held accountable for management failures.

Perhaps as important, board members who micromanage have little time left for reform leadership. Micromanagement distracts them from their real work. "My observation as superintendent," recalls Joseph Olchefske, "was [that] the more board members engaged in deep consideration of issues of policy and strategy, the less they were tempted to micromanage" (personal communication, December 20, 2004).

Problem solving by board members to make the system perform as it should is bad; intervention by board members to make the system do what is not supposed to do is worse—in fact, it is stealing from the public. School districts are supposed to hire employees, assign principals, let contracts, assign students to programs, make discipline decisions, and in other ways manage according to standard procedures that ensure effectiveness, efficiency, and fairness to all. Attempts by board members to obtain jobs, contracts, or favors of any kind for anyone are not just micromanagement; they are corrupt acts that destroy district effectiveness and undermine democracy.

As bad as problem solving and corruption by individual board members is, there is one thing even worse: micromanagement by the full board. This sometimes happens. Boards hearing a grievance or termination appeal in their judicial function, rather than limiting themselves to ruling that policy was or was not violated by management or upholding or overruling the termination, propose solutions, sometimes mandating job assignments or reporting relationships or compensation levels. Sometimes boards, usually informally, direct a superintendent to appoint a specific person to a major job or grant a specific contract to a favored vendor, or in some other area direct a management decision.

Superintendents can resist the micromanagement of individual board members, though this is sometimes difficult. It is almost impossible for them to resist the micromanagement of the full board. In fact, if micromanagement by the full board persists, a superintendent is better off resigning. No superintendent should accept responsibility for management results without the authority to make management decisions.

Why do board members and sometimes full boards micromanage? The answer is, occasionally because they want power for themselves, but mostly because their constituents want them to. Parents and other constituents know how democracy works. They expect service from their elected officials. They expect their U.S. representatives and senators to bring home the pork and solve their problems with federal agencies.

In their campaigns for reelection, federal and state officials brag about the constituent service they have provided, and are then rewarded by the voters. Why should school board members be different? And after all, there is a long tradition of powerful individuals and interest groups getting what they want out of school districts.

Also, sometimes board members micromanage because they feel they have to; otherwise nothing gets done. Windows remain broken. Buses continue to be late. Teachers don't show up for class. Hallways aren't safe.

Superintendents who fail to manage effectively invite micromanagement. Nevertheless, board members always err when they micromanage, whether it is well intentioned or not. Micromanagement does not make things better. It may solve a problem, but it makes management dysfunctional, and for every problem a board member solves, two new ones pop up.

If superintendents are not managing, board members need to insist they put effective management systems into place or face termination. If superintendents want to reduce the temptation for board members to micromanage, they need to make certain district-management systems work. Working together to support and operate effective management systems, follow clear protocols for resolving constituent complaints, and educate the public to turn first to management for solutions to management problems is the only way for boards and superintendents to put an end to well-intentioned micromanagement.

Educating the public can take time. Some districts are so poorly managed and some communities so accustomed to viewing board members as problem solvers that improved management and effective protocols must be accompanied by communication plans. Board members are the district's most effective communicators with their constituents. They should take every opportunity at public meetings and in private conversations to emphasize their role as policy makers rather than problem solvers.

Board members can also reduce the opportunity for micromanagement through their actions, for example, keeping unannounced visits to schools to a minimum. In fact, though attendance at as many school events as possible is a plus, unannounced visits are a distinct minus. Principals can easily assume a hidden agenda, and offhand comments, even compliments regarding procedures, programs, decorations, and so on, can be interpreted as management suggestions.

Well-intentioned micromanagement can be stopped, by effective and responsive management systems, by constituent education, by clear protocols for handling complaints, by vigorous responses from superintendents when individual board members cross the line, and by the collective weight of the board falling hard on board members who have difficulty breaking bad habits. As for corrupt board members, the superintendent and board colleagues must shine the public spotlight on every attempt to obtain special favors. When this does not work, boards should publicly censure colleagues and, if the situation warrants it, ask for help from the state education agency or make a referral to the district attorney.

MANAGEMENT OVERSIGHT

Good board members and effective boards do not micromanage, but they are trustees for the public. They must accept responsibility for establishing and maintaining high ethical standards for themselves and all district employees. They must ensure that everyone follows the law in letter and spirit. This means ethics codes, conflict-of-interest policies, equal opportunity for employment and contracts, transparency, periodic monitoring of business and academic-performance indicators, periodic reviews of major management systems, periodic reviews of internal audit procedures, and annual external financial audits. In short, this means management oversight.

Management oversight is a major board responsibility. Management oversight, however, is not management. Some boards, in their zeal to oversee management, get entangled in management, slowing decision making, disempowering their superintendent, and undermining overall management effectiveness. This is most often the case where management has in the past, perhaps under a previous superintendent, demonstrated incompetence, neglect, or even malfeasance.

How do boards cross this line? Most often, they do so through board committees. Standing committees are established in such areas as finance, budget, facilities, and personnel. These committees meet regularly, often monthly, and dig into the fine points of money management, budget monitoring and adjustments, contracts and contract management, and the hiring, compensation, discipline, transfer, and termination of employees. Board members become experts in these areas, or at least they think they do.

They also establish close working relationships with the superintendent's direct reports. This can be dangerous. Board members inevitably become acquainted with and often friends of Central Office administrators and some principals. But it is not wise for them to discuss business with district employees, with the exception of the superintendent's direct reports. And even these conversations should be shared with the superintendent at the earliest opportunity. A board member's observation or opinion can come across to a Central Office administrator or principal as a directive. Working relationships between board members and direct reports can easily lead to management relationships.

For these and other reasons, a committee established to review management results can easily become a committee to review management decisions, and soon board members may even start to share their opinions about upcoming management decisions. The committee may not be officially making management recommendations, but board member opinions about past decisions powerfully influence future decisions, and opinions about decisions not yet made become directives. At this point the board committee has become, in effect, a management committee, undermining the superintendent's management authority and weakening the overall management of the district.

This is not management oversight. This is management. Management oversight is not influencing management decisions before they are made. It is not even reviewing management decisions after they are made. It is guaranteeing the integrity of major management systems and processes and reviewing results.

There is a way for boards to do this through a combination of board workshops and superintendent reports or, if the board wishes, management audits by external auditors. To start the process, the board gives the superintendent adequate notice—at least 2 months—to prepare a workshop to educate the board and the public on a major business operation, say, construction management or human resource management. At the workshop, the superintendent and his or her staff, using documents and visual displays of data, explain such things as how the system is structured, how the major processes work, how nonroutine decisions are made, the use of performance measures, and the effectiveness of internal checks and balances.

Board members, thoroughly prepared for the workshop, have an opportunity to ask questions, request policy recommendations from the superintendent to remedy policy gaps, and make suggestions. For example, board members might request policies to properly vet candidates for employment, set maximum and minimum compensation levels for job positions, or govern financial-portfolio management. They might suggest alternative or additional performance measures, point out deficiencies in administrative procedures, and outline the time line and format for reports to the board on system performance. The superintendent will have no difficulty recognizing which suggestions have broad board support.

Once management has responded with an initial report on systems changes and the board has approved the requested policy changes, the board can confidently rely on annual reports from the superintendent (or where there has been a pattern of abuse or public interest is high, quarterly reports from the superintendent and annual performance audits from external firms) to assure itself that all is well. At this point, with rare exceptions, board members should consider the subject closed until reports are due.

Board members can now respond to constituent and media questions about operations in the area, confident that they understand how the system works, that internal checks and balances are in place, that performance measures are being collected, and that annually they and the public will receive a full report. They can assure constituents who have questions that when the superintendent submits his or her annual report, the board may consider improvements or increased oversight. Meanwhile, the superintendent, knowing how performance will be judged, is free to manage within the policies set by the board for a full year without distracting questions or requests for information. This is oversight of management without micromanagement.

Good information presented to the board in a timely manner is the key to management oversight, policy oversight (considered in Chapter 7), and the board's ultimate responsibility for district performance in all its manifestations. With relevant information, boards know how well systems, policies, and programs are working; where management should concentrate its efforts; where resources are needed; about trends that indicate future problems; how well schools are performing compared to other like schools in the district and state; and what the public believes about its schools. Without relevant information a board is steering blind.

An important point needs to be made about information. Information is definite knowledge, which means it must be based on more than opinion. It must be based on data. And the data must be accurate, timely, and relevant. Accuracy and timeliness are sometimes difficult to determine. Relevancy can be a huge challenge.

Relevancy frequently is determined by changing circumstances or assumptions. Consider test scores or the drop-out rate. Student achievement on the state assessment may drop because the passing standard was raised or the test made more difficult. The high school completion rate may go down because the state is no longer counting the GED Equivalency test as high school completion.

Board members must understand the context and assumptions that support data, have confidence in the reliability of the data collection systems, have reason to believe that the data they receive is accurate and timely, and see the relevancy of the data to the question at hand. This work is not easy. Where superintendents don't provide boards with an education on district information systems and a dashboard for monitoring district performance, boards should request such. If such is not forthcoming, the board should establish an information advisory committee of community professionals to assist them and request external audits of information systems.

One last point about information: Boards should demand that data be presented so that it can be easily understood. Lengthy budget documents, financial statements, and evaluation reports are, by themselves, of little value. Boards should demand that these documents and all other information presented to them be summarized visually in charts and graphs and that board members be given an opportunity to ask questions of those who prepared them. In order to govern, boards need comparative, longitudinal, and relevant data that is accurate, timely, and formatted visually for easy comprehension. Anything less is insufficient.

Julian Treviño, who, in addition to serving as president of the San Antonio board, owns a restaurant, captures the essence of board oversight this way: "We all know you can't improve what you don't measure. Good chefs taste everything they cook. Good boards taste performance" (personal communication, December 24, 2004).

FOLLOW OR LEAD?

One of the most difficult challenges for board members is the ultimate question for all elected officials: Do I follow public opinion or lead it? It is a question as old as democracy. Reform governance comes down firmly on the side of lead.

Leadership is a role, responsibility, and relationship issue that transcends parents, special interests, and voters generally. Board members are under tremendous pressure to do what influential voices and active voters want. For some board members, this means protecting those with privilege who benefit from the status quo or favoring a powerful interest group. For some it means advancing an ethnic agenda. Many urban board members believe they must follow the lead of the active elements in their community. They call this representation. Board members, however, must represent more than those with influence, even all those who vote. They must represent children, the broader interests of the communities they serve, even the interests of children and citizens yet unborn.

Reform governance is change governance. The way things are is a close approximation of the way those with power and influence want them to be. Board members content to reflect public opinion are not likely to be effective reform leaders.

Many voices demand improved schools. Public opinion polls show again and again that improving education is a high priority for the American people, and almost everyone agrees that urban districts cannot be allowed to continue as they are. School reform is right up there with motherhood and apple pie. But when major reforms are offered, opposition appears. Reasons multiply to defend the status quo.

Board and superintendent reformers have heard them all. The most common is, How do we know the reforms will work? We don't. No legislative body knows that new legislation will make things better. No business knows that a new product, service, or location will be successful. Leaders don't have the gift of prophecy. They act on information, experience, tried and tested judgment, and calculated risk. District reform leaders do not know for certain how proposed reforms will work. They know, however, that the current system for educating urban children is not working for all children.

Board members are representatives. They cannot ignore public opinion. But they are also trustees. They have been given the authority to lead, and lead they must. They have an obligation to understand the complexities of urban school reform at a level well beyond that of their most informed constituents. They have an obligation to read, travel, and think so that they can understand, explain, and lead.

Leading change is seldom without pain. This was certainly Ron Ottinger's experience in San Diego:

> As board president in San Diego for more terms than any other board
> president in the history of the district, I was determined to be a
> change agent and lead the transformation of San Diego City Schools
> from a district focused on process and site-based management to one
> rooted in student-achievement results and instruction. It turned out to

be a lonely path because as a result of the necessary battles along the way, more often than not friends were lost and relationships frayed. (Personal communication, December 21, 2004)

Overseeing incremental change is difficult. Good governance is always a challenge. But board members who commit themselves to managed instruction, performance/empowerment, managed performance/empowerment, a charter district, or something even more radical are in for the rides of their lives. Reform governance is not for the faint of heart.

More often than not, however, leadership prevails. Looking back on her years as board president in Duval County, Wilkinson concludes: "Board members who supported good decisions and effective policies and clearly articulated their positions generally gained the respect of their constituents and support for their positions" (personal communication, January 4, 2005).

I have found this to be true almost everywhere. Urban district reform leaders sometimes make a huge difference for children, almost always leave districts better than they found them, and generally earn the respect of community leaders.

CHAPTER 6

Building Blocks of Reform Governance

A CLEAR UNDERSTANDING OF ROLES, responsibilities, and relationships is the foundation of reform governance. Resting directly on this foundation box in the Reform Governance Framework is a box labeled Building Blocks of Reform Governance (Figure 6.1). This box represents the major processes by which the board does its work. Without effective processes, reform governance is difficult, maybe impossible.

Board meetings, board workshops, board committees, and the structure and process by which board members deliver constituent services are the major processes by which the board does its work. The building blocks of reform governance begin with at least these four elements. There are others that are also important, such as convening annual retreats, evaluating the superintendent, building relationships with community elites, holding town hall meetings, responding to media questions, meeting with newspaper editorial boards, and attending state and national conventions. But these four are the major reoccurring activities the public sees, and these are the ones where board members act most decisively.

BOARD MEETINGS

Board meetings are the time and place at which the board acts, and what the public sees at board meetings largely determines what the public thinks of the board. Effective board meetings are the first prerequisite for reform governance. Frequent, long, unfocused, or contentious meetings are sure signs of an ineffective, perhaps even dysfunctional, board. Everything matters, including length, time of day, agenda, protocol, and configuration of the room.

As Rick Hess explains:

> Board meetings send clear signals to various audiences, including system employees, parents, local officials, and the local media. Crisp, efficient, well-ordered meetings send the signal that the board knows its business and is taking its stewardship of the schools seriously. Late

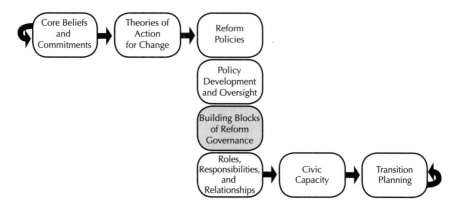

Figure 6.1. Building blocks of reform governance as element of Reform Governance Framework.

or disorganized meetings, personal conflict, or rambling discussions suggest to observers that a board is lacking clear direction. This can undermine support for reform measures and encourage dissension and resistance within the district. (Personal communication, December 21, 2004)

Ron Ottinger reports that San Diego's school board meetings used to be almost completely dysfunctional:

There was no ending time; board members could speak as long and as often as they liked on any agenda item, and protests and disruptions in the board auditorium were not only tolerated but often encouraged by individual board members. Finally, the board majority got smart, researched how other large urban districts and city elected bodies operated, and changed the board's bylaws to bring order to board meetings. In addition, as board president, I brought in a parliamentarian to instruct the board in the procedures of Robert's Rules of Order, which significantly reduced clashes, gamesmanship, and disruption by board members and the public at board meetings. (Personal communication, December 21, 2004)

There is no one pattern for effective board meetings. Cities, like people, have personalities. Boards have traditions. What works for one board may not work for another. Every board meeting is context specific. Further, the same board may vary meetings from time to time for specific purposes. Nevertheless, there are practice patterns that contribute to effective meetings. Boards should consider these before adopting something different.

Frequency, Length, and Content

Frequency. Boards should hold fewer rather than more regular business meetings: under most circumstances, one a month is sufficient. Board meetings are a tremendous drain on the time of superintendents and senior administrators. Reform boards want their superintendent and senior staff working to improve student achievement and district operations, not constantly getting ready for and following up on board meetings. Board member time is also important. Most board members are part-time public servants with family and work responsibilities.

Length. Meetings should seldom be more than 3 hours in length and should never go late into the night. Long meetings not only consume an inordinate amount of time, but also encourage the board to micromanage and are often a sign of bad planning. Furthermore, board members make poor decisions when fatigued and under the stress of late-night meetings. With proper agenda management, a board can transact necessary business with one short meeting a month. Long board meetings are not necessary for effective governance.

Content. Even in short meetings, there should be time for recognizing and honoring excellence—in students, employees, or others who have achieved distinction as scholars, artists, athletes, teachers, volunteers, or community leaders. Shining the spotlight on excellence builds district morale and public support. Public recognition should be short and highly scripted.

Regular business meetings might also include reports from the superintendent. This is an excellent time for the superintendent to educate the board, the workforce, and the community about important achievements, programs, issues, or plans. And reports give board members an opportunity to make comments, helping to set the tone for the district and the community. For example, a report on the effectiveness of a new literacy program or NCLB educates the workforce and the public, and the board response sets the tone for how the board wants the workforce and the public to respond.

The board should consider no more than four priority items for discussion and approval at a board meeting. These items should be selected for importance, because they require board deliberation, or to educate the workforce and the public. They should be professionally presented and thoroughly debated.

The rest of the items should be grouped together for approval with one vote. This division of the agenda into a priority agenda and a consent agenda enables the board to quickly approve numerous routine items with one vote and then probe deeply into a few major issues. Of course, individual board members may pull one or more items out of the consent agenda for separate approval because they wish to highlight the issue, seek clarification, propose an amendment, or vote against a measure. No problem. A board is a democratic body, and individual opinions are part of the democratic process.

Agenda Preparation and Review

Agenda Preparation. Infrequent, short board meetings, with most routine items grouped into a consent agenda, require careful planning. Agreement and consistency on agenda preparation, agenda format, and an agenda-review process is essential. Agenda preparation should be a shared responsibility. Board presidents (because it is a board meeting) and superintendents (because they need board approval so the district can act on a wide range of issues) share this responsibility. As a practical matter, the superintendent usually proposes the agenda, but should obtain the approval of the board president before sending out the agenda; and the board president should not surprise the superintendent with agenda items. Board policy should make possible the addition of agenda items by signature of a small number of board members.

Agenda items and staff reports should follow a standard format that highlights significant points, for example, reference to relevant policies, estimated costs, budget category, labor contract, and so on. Boards should insist on receiving data in visual displays, as mentioned above. Reports should be short; when they are long, executive summaries should be provided.

Agenda Review. An agenda review process gives board members the opportunity to review with relevant senior administrators all agenda items, seek clarification, point out problems, or voice opposition. It enables board members to come to meetings prepared to thoughtfully discuss priority items and quickly approve most items in a consent agenda. The process begins with distribution of the agenda to board members well in advance of the meeting. A week is ideal. Four days is minimal. There are several ways to conduct the review: scheduled conversations between board members and senior members of the superintendent's staff, board committees, or posted meetings of the board as a committee of the whole.

Duval's Wilkinson prefers committees of the whole. "Agenda review meetings," she says, "are very important for moving forward in an orderly manner the business of the district. Boards should have regularly scheduled meetings of the board as a committee of the whole so that all board members are aware of all issues and the concerns of individual board members" (personal communication, January 4, 2005).

Board members who do not avail themselves of the agenda-review process and then waste the board's time at board meetings with numerous questions should be put under considerable peer pressure to follow the prescribed practice and should be reminded openly at board meetings that they had ample opportunity to get their questions answered before the meeting.

Agenda review also enables the superintendent to discern problems that board members have with agenda items. No superintendent can perfectly anticipate board member reactions to agenda items, and sometimes superintendents bring flawed items to the board. Agenda review enables superintendents to pull or modify items or at least go into the board meeting knowing what to expect. Julian Treviño states that in his experience in San Antonio, "superintendents and senior staff welcome agenda review sessions. They see how the board reacts to items and have enough time to make revisions as needed" (personal communication, December 24, 2004).

Neither superintendents nor board members like surprises at the board table. Agenda review ensures that that there will be none and vastly increases the probability that the meeting will be productive for the district and make the board and the superintendent look good.

Meeting Management

Configuration. Board meetings are best held around a crescent-shaped table facing long tables for senior staff. A crescent-shaped table facilitates discussion among board members—the primary purpose of the meeting—and facing tables for senior staff places the people who are most likely to have answers to board member questions directly in front of the board. The superintendent most appropriately sits at the board table, signifying his or her position as a colleague and de facto member of the governing team.

Opening Statement. Because the primary purpose of regular business meetings is the efficient transaction of board business, it is useful for the board president to open meetings with a formal statement that outlines the board's powers and responsibilities (govern, not manage), the purpose of the meeting (recognize excellence, receive reports, approve policies and contracts, not solve management problems), and the rules and processes followed by the board to facilitate orderly decision making (parliamentary procedure, courteous discourse, fairness). This statement helps to focus the board and educate the public and sets the tone for the meeting.

Treviño reports that San Antonio opens regular board meetings; citizen presentations; and closed, or executive, sessions with prepared statements. "We rotate the reading of these statements among board members. Board members enjoy doing this, for it helps keep them as well as the public focused on purpose and expectations" (personal communication, December 24, 2004).

Decorum. Customs vary from district to district, but all things considered, business attire and formal speech—last names, not first—enhance the dignity of the board and demonstrate to the public the importance of the board's work. Do legislators or judges wear casual clothes to work?

Tempo and tone are important. Boards should neither appear rushed nor stray from the agenda. Adequate time should be given to the superintendent and his or her staff to make presentations and answer questions. All board members should be allowed adequate and equal opportunity to speak, and no board member should be allowed to dominate debate. In addition, all interactions among board members should be respectful. Board members should always act as if their colleagues are honest in their opinions, even if they are obviously grandstanding or advancing a personal or special interest agenda.

Public Participation. A board meeting is a meeting of the board in public, not a public meeting. Public seating should underscore the fact that members of the public are viewers, not participants. Ideally, the board meets in a formal boardroom, with the public in facing seats.

Public comment on agenda items during the business meeting or general comments following the conduct of business should be welcome. Public comment gives citizens an opportunity to be heard. But citizens should be required to sign up in advance, time per speaker and topic should be limited, and the board should demand respectful address and not allow interruptions or applause. Neither should board members engage in discussions with citizens or try to solve problems. The board president should simply thank citizens for their comments and refer problems to management.

Wise boards are prepared for intemperate citizens and unruly crowds. Board members should never show approval for invective or threats, lack of support for rulings of the chair, or anger or fear when faced with insults or intimidation. Discreet or visible security, according to circumstances, should always be present, and plans for crowd control should be in place if there is an expectation that this might be necessary.

The public owns the public schools, and from time to time the board should provide citizens with a formal opportunity to speak at length to the entire board on various issues or on a hot pending issue. But there is a right time, right place, and right way to conduct public hearings. The right time is not at regular business meetings of the board of education. Public hearings should be scheduled, perhaps in different venues around the district, to consider specific districtwide or neighborhood issues—such as redistricting board seats, redrawing school attendance boundaries, or building programs. And board members should listen—and perhaps from time to time ask a question for clarification—but never debate.

Television. One additional point: television. There are pros and cons to televising board meetings. It is an excellent way to inform the public. It also encourages grandstanding by board members and citizens. Boards should be thoughtful about this decision.

Duval County's Wilkinson points out that some communities expect televised meetings:

> Where this is expected, the board chairman and the superintendent should plan the meeting with extra care; board members should commit to limiting the time individual members have to speak on an issue; and the board chairman should firmly enforce the rules. (Personal communication, January 4, 2005)

JUDICIAL HEARINGS

Boards meet not only in regular business sessions and at public hearings. In most states, boards rule on employee grievances and terminations. At judicial hearings, it is important for the board to have its own legal counsel. The district and the board do not have the same interest. The employee acts as appellant, the district acts as appellee, and the board acts as the court of appeals.

In fact, the district and the board have different interests on other occasions. Prime examples are state sunshine laws, ethics codes, and issues regarding elections and campaign finance. These are board, not district, issues. Wise boards retain experienced school attorneys to advise them on these matters.

The rules for board members in judicial hearings are follow the law, do your homework, show respect to all, don't discuss matters under deliberation outside the hearing, and be fair. These points should be obvious to all.

A less obvious but equally important point for boards is to never mandate administrative action in judicial decisions. A board, in its judicial capacity, determines whether an employee is terminated or whether an employee grievance is sustained. It is not the board's role, as mentioned above, to respond to termination or grievance appeals by mandating management structures or processes, job assignments, compensation, or anything else that is rightfully the responsibility of management.

BOARD WORKSHOPS

Board workshops are a powerful tool for exercising management oversight, as seen in Chapter 5, and for driving a reform agenda. A board workshop is a posted 3- to 4-hour meeting of the board for the purpose of exploring in depth a particular subject. The superintendent and his or her staff present in great detail information about a management system, a significant issue facing the district, or a major reform policy option. No recommendations are made. No actions are taken. The board simply listens, and board members respond with questions and comments. But the consequences are profound.

"Board workshops and retreats were incredibly productive sessions for our board and for me and my staff in Seattle," states former superintendent Olchefske. "These sessions gave us a significant, unbroken span of time to raise our perspective off of the 'here and now' and explore in depth major issues requiring strategies with long horizons" (personal communication, December 20, 2004).

Why are workshops so powerful? Because they make clear to the superintendent and the community what is important to the board; because they educate the board and community about big issues; because they enable the board to exercise management oversight without micromanaging; and because they serve as a springboard for major policy development.

Effective workshop management begins with a decision by the board, perhaps at an annual offsite retreat, to schedule three to five workshops aligned with the board's strategic priorities during the following year. Quarterly meetings make good sense. Boards might also want to leave open one date for quick response to an unexpected opportunity.

The board should make clear to the superintendent that it expects a professional presentation, which, if appropriate, should be complete with PowerPoint, handouts, and abundant data presented visually. Research reports for advance reading might also be appropriate. And board members should come prepared.

Just by scheduling the workshop, the board informs the superintendent and announces to the community that it considers the subject a high priority for the district. It also forces the superintendent and his or her senior staff to master a complex topic, distill the salient points, and develop data to support current practices or policy options. Few superintendents will fail to meet this challenge.

Moreover, few superintendents will fail to learn something in the process. Most presentations on a current situation, for example, the operation of a major management system or instructional program, will include announcements that some management structures or practices have already been changed and that others are anticipated. Just by holding the workshop, the board drives improvements in operations.

It also receives an education. Effective governance for oversight or change is based on knowledge about what is and is not possible. The best classroom for a board is a board workshop, and the best teacher—assuming the board has hired a reform leader as superintendent—is the superintendent.

The public also needs knowledge. If it is to have confidence in current operations, it needs to know how things work. If it is going to support change, it needs to know what options for change are available and how the district can learn from the research literature and the experiences of other districts.

For this reason, board workshops, unlike board retreats, should be staged as media events.

If board workshops did nothing more than push management to reexamine operations and programs and educate the board and the public, they would have value, but the real power of the workshop is what follows. Through workshops, boards can exercise their management oversight responsibility and provide reform leadership.

Management oversight has already been examined. Workshops for reform leadership look much the same. The board requests the superintendent to present a workshop on curriculum and professional development, district accountability systems, weighted student funding, district charter schools, or whatever major reform initiative advances the board's theory of action.

At the workshop, the superintendent and his or her staff educate the board and the public about how the district currently operates in this area, the research literature, and the experiences of other districts. Perhaps the superintendent also outlines the policy changes, structure, staffing, training, cost, and time that would be required to create and implement change. Board members ask questions and by their comments demonstrate whether they want to move forward. If they do, the stage for action is set.

At this point the board has options on how to proceed. It can ask the superintendent to prepare policy recommendations or appoint a blue ribbon commission of citizens and district employees to prepare policy recommendations; or it can determine that the best method for policy development is an ad hoc board committee or a board committee of the whole.

The pros and cons of these various methods of policy development will be considered in Chapter 7. The point here is simply to describe how board workshops can be used by the board of education to drive a reform agenda.

BOARD COMMITTEES

Most boards have committees. Standing committees, ad hoc committees, and committees of the whole all have their places as effective tools for effective governance. Standing committees can be effective vehicles for facilitating the board's work, but they also can be bottlenecks for decision making and encourage micromanagement. They should be used with great care. Ad hoc committees are especially useful for policy development. And committees of the whole are ideal for agenda review and reaching consensus on board processes.

Standing Committees

Large legislative bodies could not function without standing committees. Committees gather information, dig deeply into issues, and prepare exact language for legislation. Legislators on standing committees become experts in the complex details of policy. Without this expertise, legislatures would make a mess of legislation.

School boards are quite different. Typically legislatures have scores of members, and committees can fairly reflect the balance of power in the body. Most school boards have seven to nine members. It is difficult for standing board committees to reflect the balance of power on the board. For this reason, board committees can easily become bottlenecks, stalling full board consideration of important items.

Consider a board of nine with four standing committees: instruction, finance, personnel, and facilities. Given the need to spread committee assignments fairly among all board members, the three or four members on any of these committees might not reflect the reform commitment or political center of the board. Policy or contract items referred to such a committee for review could easily become stuck there, depriving the board of an opportunity to act in a timely manner.

Also, standing board committees encourage board members to develop intimate knowledge of district operations and close relationships with senior management, increasing the risk of micromanagement. If, for example, three board members meet often with senior administrators to review policies and major actions in the area of personnel, with growing knowledge and friendship will come a growing temptation to offer management advice, which can quickly become micromanagement. In fact, as described in Chapter 5, some boards even design standing committees to become management committees.

Cognizant of these issues, Julian Treviño reports that the San Antonio board has only one standing committee, a Futures Committee. "We use our one standing committee, the Futures Committee, to explore future critical issues and potential problems. In addition, the superintendent uses the committee as a sounding board for possible initiatives" (personal communication, December 24, 2004).

The downsides of standing committees are not inevitable. Some boards use standing committees with great success. Where boards are unified, where all board members are invited to attend standing committees, or where standing committees mostly receive information from the superintendent and serve an agenda-review function rather than a policy development or oversight function, standing committees are less likely to be problematic. Boards that want to govern through standing committees should keep these principles in mind.

There is one standing committee that no board should do without: an audit committee. Even if not required by state law, a standing audit committee—perhaps assisted by an advisory panel of audit professionals from the community—enables the board to properly exercise its fiduciary responsibility in the critical area of finance. Boards should approve the district's internal audit structure and process and review internal audits. (The internal auditor should report to the superintendent, but the board should get all internal audit reports, except in the case of investigations that require confidentiality.) Boards should also oversee the external audit process. It is difficult for boards to carry out these responsibilities without a standing audit committee, and to neglect them courts disaster.

Ad Hoc Committees and Committees of the Whole

Ad Hoc Committees. Ad hoc committees of the board are established to accomplish a specific objective, normally to bring a recommendation to the full board. They cease to exist when their work is completed. Appointment by the board president is the preferred method of establishment. This avoids conflict over membership. All board members should have a standing invitation to attend all meetings. This enhances board knowledge and diminishes opposition at the board table. The superintendent may be asked to assign district employees (to provide expertise), and the board president may invite community leaders (to provide community input) to sit with the committee as nonvoting members.

Ad hoc committees are created to focus on a specific issue, have a well-defined objective, and meet regularly for a specified period of time. They are an excellent method for policy development. (The pros and cons of using them for this purpose are outlined in Chapter 7.) The full board should approve a written charter for all committees, stating clearly the desired output, time frame, and limitations. Committees must understand, for example, that they cannot command the time of district personnel except as authorized by the superintendent.

Committees of the Whole. For some issues, boards may want to meet in a committee of the whole. Committees of the whole need not be chaired by the board president, and they differ from board workshops or hearings in that the board is not receiving a presentation from the superintendent (except when used for agenda review) or input from the public. Rather the full board is meeting as a committee to resolve an issue.

Committees of the whole can be used to develop policy, but normally ad hoc committees do this more efficiently. However, there is probably no better way for a board to reach consensus on the building blocks of reform governance than to meet in a committee of the whole. Everything covered in this chapter—board meetings, board workshops, board committees, and the provision of administrative services to board members—as well as other issues, such as defining the powers of the board president or agreeing on protocols for responding to media inquiries, requires the consensus of the full board. Reaching agreement on these protocols and practices is an essential first step for effective governance. Time spent in this work is time well spent.

ADMINISTRATIVE SUPPORT

Board Member Needs

Serving on a large urban board is time consuming. Board members must attend meetings, participate in workshops, and serve on committees, and they must read scores of pages of agenda items and supporting materials to be ready for these events. And this is just the tip of the iceberg.

One significant time-consuming activity of an urban board member is constituent service. Time may vary depending on the overall efficiency and effectiveness of district operations. If systems don't work as they should, a board member can receive up to 20 phone calls or e-mails a week from constituents with legitimate complaints about unavailable textbooks, undisciplined classrooms, ineffective teaching, overcrowded schools, inadequate parking, broken windows, bus schedules, pupil-transfer decisions, and other problems. Even if the district operations are premier, given the sensitive nature of the work, board members will from time to time hear from unhappy parents or constituents.

In addition, numerous ceremonial occasions require attendance: programs, luncheons, and dinners honoring organizations and people; school concerts, plays, holiday programs, fairs, and PTO meetings; sports events (Friday night football if you live in Texas); and city events such as quarterly luncheon meetings of the chamber of commerce. Board members don't actually have to attend all these events, but wise ones attend as many as they can, for this is how knowledge is gained, networks are built and maintained, and civic capacity is bolstered to support the district and the board's reform agenda.

Finally, if a board member wants to be a board leader, numerous conversations with the superintendent and breakfast or luncheon meetings with colleagues or civic leaders are required to build relationships and support for ideas—leadership is all about relationships and the power of ideas. Then there are national and state school board conventions and from time to time the need to lobby state legislators. Few board members can do what must be done in less than 20 hours a week. If everything that could be done were done, board service would be a full-time job.

Board Services Work

Board service is public service. Most urban board members serve without pay or receive only a nominal amount to compensate them for their time in board meetings. How can people with families and jobs find time to serve effectively on an urban board? The short answer is, they cannot without sacrificing career or family. The longer answer is that a highly effective board services office can make the work much less time consuming and enhance the professionalism of the board. Board members need help with management of events, records, communications, scheduling, correspondence, and constituent service. Administrative support from a professional board services department is one of the essential building blocks of reform governance.

Every board meeting and every board event must be planned and executed to the highest standards of events management. Board minutes, agenda documents, board committee minutes, mailing lists, and all documents must be managed to the highest standards of professional records management. All incoming phone calls, e-mails, and other communications to board members must be handled with the same care they receive in the superintendent's office. Everyone who calls should receive a response.

Board members receive numerous invitations to events and have busy schedules. Board services must track invitations, provide RSVPs for board members, supply information on dress and directions to board members, and in every way possible make certain that board members know when and where they are supposed to be and that they arrive prepared for what is expected of them.

What about phone calls and correspondence? Board members cannot respond personally to every phone call, letter, or e-mail. Board services should have professionals who know how to respond to phone calls and ghostwrite responses under the supervision required by individual board members.

One of the most important responsibilities of board services is assisting board members with constituent service. Constituent service is time consuming and must be done right. Board members cannot be expected to respond to every complaint. Whatever protocol the board-superintendent team establishes for constituent service management, significant administrative support will be required.

Board Services Staff

In small to medium-size districts, the superintendent's administrative support staff frequently supports the board. But board members in large urban districts need the support of a professional board services office. Professional personnel and fine-tuned systems are a prerequisite for a high-functioning board.

As a rule, a professional board services staff of three to six serving all board members (with staff members cross-trained so that each can on short notice do whatever needs to be done) is preferred to board members having individual staff. It is less expensive and service is always available when needed. Further, individual staff members have a tendency to become constituent problem solvers and pull the board member they serve into micromanagement.

The board services staff should be district employees and report to the superintendent or a senior district administrator. Board staff members who are employees of the board are too easily tempted to enter into turf battles with the superintendent. The best model is for board staff to serve board members as clients rather than employers. The model for board services staff in relation to the superintendent and board members should be similar to that of in-house lawyers in major corporations who report upward to the general counsel but are assigned company executives as clients.

Board members should, of course, participate in developing job descriptions, regulating the flow of work, and evaluating performance. It is the board president's job to coordinate the work of the office to ensure equity of service for all board members.

Research and Policy Work

Board members will note one support function that reform governance recommends not be assigned to the board services staff: analysis of research and policy. Boards need support in this area. As Duval's Wilkinson puts it, "It is essential that boards have access to professional research staff to introduce them to the literature on education policy and help them understand research, and identify best practices" (personal communication, January 4, 2005).

Research and policy work for the board, however, is best done by the research staff of the district. Independent research and policy work for the board by a small board services staff is likely to be inadequate. Duplicating the district's research department is wasteful. And in any case, the superintendent needs to be in this loop. Policy work is the work of the board-superintendent team.

The same process used by board members to place items on the agenda for regular business meetings or to request legal opinions should be used to request research or policy work: Board members should make requests through the board president, and if the president refuses, a signed request by a minority of the board should trigger action. Boards should, without hesitation, request research and policy work when needed; and the superintendent should always enthusiastically respond. Boards and superintendents need to learn together.

CONCLUSION

Board meetings, workshops, committees, and board services are the major building blocks required for effective governance, whether reform governance or more traditional good governance. There are other important and repeatable processes used by boards to carry out their work, as mentioned at the beginning of this chapter, but these are the key ones that absolutely have to work well.

Regular business meetings of the board are where the board acts, exercising its governance power and conducting the public's business. Workshops are where the board works, overseeing management and driving a reform agenda. Committees of the whole, ad hoc committees, and standing committees are where the board reaches consensus on processes, solves board problems, develops policy, and regulates the flow of board business. And the board services staff supports all these board functions as well as the individual work of board members. If these processes don't work well, boards cannot govern and they cannot lead.

Establishing effective processes for the board's work, like clarifying roles and responsibilities and building positive working relationships, is a foundation for reform governance.

CHAPTER 7

Policy Development and Oversight

REFORM POLICY DEVELOPMENT, APPROVAL, and oversight should be the primary work of an urban school board, and policy content should be the primary output of a board's work. Policy content is driven by the board's core beliefs and theory of action and rests on productive relationships, the major processes by which the board does its work, and the correct application of the methods and principles of policy development and oversight.

In the two previous chapters I have examined relationships and processes. In this chapter I examine policy development and oversight, the second box in the central column of the Reform Governance Framework and the box that supports policy content (see Figure 7.1).

POLICY CONTEXT

What are policies and how do they fit within the overall framework of actions taken by school boards? Policies are documents approved by the board that outline goals, standards, or principles to guide or prescribe actions and constrain behavior by district employees, students, and others who interact with the district.

Boards act when they vote, and they vote on many things other than policy recommendations. Boards approve budgets, financial audits, contracts with vendors, the sale or purchase of property, the acceptance of gifts and grants, personnel changes (in most districts), legislative agendas, school names, superintendent evaluations, and much more. Few of these actions establish policy, but all are vital governance actions.

Boards also approve goals and plans. As noted above, policies can precede or follow goals and plans: precede if they are major policies that require strategic plans for implementation; follow if they are minor policies that are required to implement a strategic plan. Goals and plans can also precede or follow each other. Broad goals, like the board's commitments, require strategic plans for their achievement. However, many plans include goals as milestones to mark achievement. Clarity on a theory of action provides the foundation for goal setting and planning.

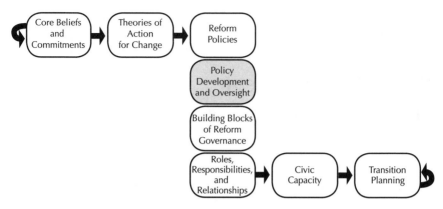

Figure 7.1. Policy development and oversight as element of Reform Governance Framework.

Goal setting and planning is a shared board-superintendent responsibility. Boards must approve goals and plans, and they should involve their communities in the development of broad goals. But boards should rely heavily on their superintendents for advice on numerical goals or time frames. Superintendents have a much better grasp of what is achievable. However, because some superintendents are reluctant to put a lot of pressure on the system, boards should insist on stretch goals.

Stress is not bad: Without it, few people or organizations perform to capacity. Too much stress, however, is counterproductive. Superintendents have better insight than boards into how much stress the organization can take and are better positioned to set realistic milestones for performance. Unrealistic goals are not credible with the workforce or the public and failure to reach them undermines the credibility of the board. Establishing stretch but doable goals requires board-superintendent negotiations based on trust and experience.

Plans at the strategic level—which major reform policies should be developed this year—are board led and superintendent approved. But operating plans and the budgets that support them are the superintendent's responsibility to produce and the board's responsibility to modify as necessary and approve. Obviously, effective planning requires board-superintendent trust and benefits greatly from experience gained by a board-superintendent team working together for several years.

In short, boards do many important things at the board table besides approve policies. Policies, however, are integrally related to most other board actions, and they are the most powerful levers available to boards for transforming districts. They are the laws of the land for the district. Properly implemented, they determine what district employees and those who operate within the district's sphere of control do day after day in schools and everywhere else that the district operates.

ROUTINE OPERATING POLICIES

Policies can be separated into two groups: routine operating policies and reform policies. Routine operating policies are required to maintain stability in a changing environment. Reform policies are required to drive change.

Newly elected or appointed board members will quickly discover that their districts have policies, hundreds of them. These policies are the rules— federal, state, and district—that regulate the behavior of those who operate within the district's sphere of control. The policies may be clearly organized, coherent, and accessible or disorganized, contradictory, and impenetrable.

One of the first things newly configured boards frequently do is request a policy audit to get their policy manual in order. Most state school board associations provide models and consulting support to do this. Even with this excellent technical support, producing a useful policy manual can be difficult and labor intensive.

Of course, district policies are one thing; what people actually do is another. If a district has incoherent and contradictory policies, this is a problem for the board. If policies are clear but ignored by the workforce, this is a job for the superintendent.

Typically, an urban board approves 10 to 20 policies each year, perhaps 90% or more of which are routine operating policies. These are policies required to establish sound operating systems and, when systems are stable, make changes to enable the district to continue doing what it has been doing in a changing environment. Operating policies are important; they establish and maintain stability. It is an iron law of organizations that stability is required before meaningful change can be accomplished. Where chaos reigns, change has no meaning.

A district with dysfunctional finance, accounting, payroll, budget control, information management, facilities maintenance, procurement, and other business systems, for example, needs sound operations before it can effectively act on a theory of action for improving student achievement. A district that does not have accurate and timely information on teacher qualifications and absenteeism, student attendance, student discipline, and school safety, or is unable to place textbooks in classes at the beginning of the year, quickly fill teacher vacancies, handle grievances, or file required reports to federal and state agencies is not ready to implement performance pay for teachers or promotion standards for children.

Creating and managing effective operational systems is management's work, but board policies are needed to support this work, and sometimes resistance to change is fierce. Boards faced with dysfunctional systems must be prepared to give their superintendents strong and unyielding support.

But assume stable and effective school and business operations. Boards still need to approve annually routine operating policies. Why? Because the environment is always changing. New technologies, changing demographics, or incidents that expose systems failures require new policies, not in order to fundamentally change the way the district operates, but, rather, to keep the district operating smoothly.

Consider the following examples. Cell phones become common and parents want access to their children when school lets out, so the board approves a new cell phone policy that allows students to carry cell phones, as long as they are turned off during school hours. Because some neighborhoods have aged and others have attracted young families, school-attendance-zone boundaries need to be redrawn. The board acts. Because of an incident at a school with an unruly, armed parent, the board approves a policy that requires all visitors to sign in and obtain a name badge before entering a school. Because a local television reporter has uncovered bus drivers with criminal backgrounds, the board approves a policy that requires all new and existing employees to submit to criminal background checks. One could go on and on.

Most routine operating policy changes come directly to the board as recommendations of the superintendent, though they seldom originate with the superintendent. Rather, they bubble up through the organization as frontline administrators notice that current policies do not meet the needs of changing circumstances. Most routine policies are approved as part of the consent agenda.

On occasion, responding to issues in their neighborhoods, board members initiate routine operating policies, for example, use of a district athletic field by a neighborhood sports association. The board also originates policies for regulating board behavior and processes. Examples include ethics codes, professional travel for board members, and the building block processes outlined in Chapter 6.

Usually, routine operating policies are not controversial and require little board attention. Sometimes they inflame entire communities and become all consuming. School-attendance-zone boundary changes, for example, because they determine where children go to school and sometimes affect property values, can pit one neighborhood against another and exacerbate racial tensions. School calendars can also become hot topics, with teachers wanting an early start to the school year and a long winter holiday break and parents wanting just the opposite.

None of the policy examples referenced above are policies designed to fundamentally change the operations of a district. In fact, they are just the opposite. They are policies designed to enable a district to change as little as possible in a changing environment.

REFORM POLICIES

There is no hard-and-fast division between operating policies and reform policies. Pupil assignment policies, for example, can be a response to changing demographic patterns or they can be designed with a clear academic intent. However, as a rule, it is easy to identify reform policies. They are policies designed to make significant changes in district performance, policies designed to effectuate the board's theory of action. Routine operating policies are reactive policies to maintain stability. Reform policies are proactive policies to drive change.

Examples of reform policies include the various policies required to put into place a tightly coupled instructional-management system: aligned curriculum, literacy and math coaches, professional development, formative and summative assessments, a student information management system, among others.

Reform policies required to implement performance/empowerment include a district accountability system that rates and ranks schools based on school-performance indicators, employee evaluations that link student achievement to evaluations, variable and performance pay for teachers, promotion standards for students, weighted student funding, and so on.

Creating a charter district would require a host of reform policies to regulate the content of charters and the processes for approving, monitoring, assessing, and revoking charters, as well as financial, facilities, and transportation policies needed to support the charter system.

Outsourcing and enterprise conversions might also be defined as reform policies inasmuch as they provide essential management infrastructure to support new district designs. These policies are a sample of the policies needed to transform urban districts, the subject of Chapter 8.

POLICY DEVELOPMENT METHODS

Who is responsible for policy development, the superintendent or the board? There is much confusion on this point. The literature on school governance and the education codes in the states are clear: Boards approve policies. But do boards have any responsibility for the development of policies? Many superintendents say no. Their view is that boards certainly can and frequently do modify policy recommendations, but the superintendent is the fountainhead of policy.

This view is at the root of much of the confusion about the governance-management interface. Consider what all too often happens. Board members are told repeatedly that they must stay out of management, that micromanagement is the sin of sins, and that they govern by policy and policy alone. Agreed. So they proceed to propose policies, only to be told that policy governance is defined as approving or rejecting policies recommended by the superintendent. And if they reject recommendations with any regularity, they are showing a lack of confidence in the superintendent, undermining his or her authority with the workforce, and weakening his or her power to lead. What, then, are they but rubber stamps?

Reform governance is clear on this point. Policy development is a shared responsibility between the board and superintendent, but the board has the final say. The relationship is indicated in the Reform Governance Framework. Recall that the down arrows representing the work of the board do not go below the governance/management line, but the up arrows representing the work of the superintendent penetrate the line. Policy leadership, however, is clearly above the line. It is a governance function.

Superintendents work both below and above the line. Below the line they manage without the interference of the board, though the board oversees management. Above the line, superintendents act as an essential part of the governance team. This is because good policy cannot be made without the active involvement of the superintendent or his or her designees. If policy is to direct management, policy must know what management is capable of doing.

Consider that almost all policies have some impact on budgets or personnel. And all policies must be evaluated for effectiveness. The superintendent is the only person who can judge the impact of a policy on the district's budget or its people, and he or she is the only one who can determine how a policy will align with existing structures and processes. In short, because the district is a system and any change in one part of the system can and likely will affect the entire system, only the superintendent can fairly judge the impact a policy might have on the district.

Even the most knowledgeable board does not have sufficient knowledge of the system to predict the impact of policies on budgets, personnel, and children. Even an experienced executive serving on a school board lacks this knowledge. Even if a previous superintendent served on the board, he or she would lack this knowledge. He would no longer be swimming in the river. The fish in the river feels the temperature and current of the water and senses the presence of predators. A fish no longer in the river no longer has this knowledge, for the river is always changing. This is why the superintendent, the only member of the governing team swimming in the management river, must be a partner in policy making.

But though the superintendent is part of the governance team and always at the policy-making table, governance is the responsibility of the board. And there are times when the board should be directly involved in the development of policy.

There are at least four methods for developing policy. The first is the most common: Perhaps 90% of all policies come to the board directly from the superintendent. These policy recommendations are developed by district staff as directed by the superintendent, usually following an administrative protocol for policy preparation and presentation that includes internal check-off by key administrators; cabinet review; and statements of purpose, background, projected costs, and source of funding. Most routine operating policies fall into this category. Unless there is a reason not to use this method, it is preferred. Superintendents and their staffs are professionals. They have the time and resources to do this work. And they are not likely to miss issues of policy alignment.

A second method is available if issues are controversial or benefit from broad input: recommendation by a superintendent-appointed blue ribbon committee, or task force. Superintendents can bring these recommendations directly to the board as task force recommendations; alternatively, superintendents can specify in the task force charter that the task force is advisory. This gives the superintendent the (sometimes much needed) freedom to modify the recommendations and bring them to the board as superintendent recommendations. Superintendent-appointed task forces are ideal for recommending policies regarding textbook adoption, district calendars, school-attendance boundaries, or major outsourcing contracts.

A third method for policy development is direct recommendation from the board. Normally, these recommendations come from a board committee, not an individual board member. For reasons outlined in Chapter 6, ad hoc committees, sometimes committees of the whole, are preferred to standing committees.

Occasionally, a board may want to charter its own blue ribbon committee to prepare a policy recommendation for board consideration. Such committees, because they limit the ability of the superintendent to influence the work, should be limited to issues that are entirely outside the official interest of the superintendent, such as decennial redistricting of board seats or other matters relating to board elections, board officers, or board ethics codes.

For superintendent or board-appointed task forces and board committees, written charters and adequate support staff are required. Charters set forth the purposes of proposed policies, financial or other parameters, and time frames. Superintendents write charters for superintendent-appointed task forces. Boards approve charters for board committees or board-appointed task forces. Without clear charters, task forces or committees can willfully or unwittingly go off on tangents and bring forth flawed recommendations. Charter writing is almost an art form. When boards find it necessary to write charters, they should welcome assistance from their superintendent.

As stated above, almost all policies have budget, staffing, and evaluation implications. Senior administrators, research staff, or representative principals and teachers are needed to provide essential information on these issues. Superintendents must provide all task forces and board committees with adequate staff.

For board committees and task forces of all kinds, the keys to good policy recommendations are the right people, a clear charter, and strong support staff.

Which policy development method should a board prefer? It depends. The most effective method for policy development is superintendent recommendation, not only for routine operating policies, but also for major reform policies. Board members are usually part-time, unpaid volunteers. They have limited time and expertise. The superintendent has the expertise, the staff, and the time. The easiest way for boards to obtain policy recommendations is to ask the superintendent to prepare them. Task forces are preferred for highly visible and controversial policies, whether reform policies or not, and these are, with luck, infrequent.

However, it all depends on circumstances. Consider again the distinction between routine operating policies and reform policies. Routine policies usually come to the board as superintendent recommendations, and frequently the first time that boards know about these policy recommendations is when they are presented at an agenda review. Great! The less time boards spend on routine operating policies the better.

Controversial policies designed to maintain smooth operations unfortunately can take a great deal of board time, but the less the better. Task forces appointed by the superintendent can bring forward excellent solutions that meet the needs of the district and the community. This method provides board members with excellent political cover, for boards can approve these recommendations without much negative political fallout. And really, do board members care that much—except for the fact that their constituents care—about when school starts, the length of holiday breaks, or the attendance-zone boundaries for a new school?

Reform policies are another matter. Boards should care a great deal about these. Approving them and ensuring their effective implementation is how boards change districts. Business and civic leaders, parents, and others may also care about these policies. If they don't, board members need to educate them to understand how these policies, in alignment with other reform policies, will effectuate the board's theory of action.

Boards must be intimately involved in the development of reform policies. This does not mean that they cannot ask the superintendent to prepare recommendations. In fact, this is frequently the case. It does mean, however, that they must have a clear picture of what they want the policy to accomplish, have thought through the pros and cons of various methods of policy development, and have chosen the method that best meets their needs.

At its annual retreat, a board and superintendent might determine that two major reform policies should be developed during the year. They might decide that the superintendent should bring forward one as a superintendent's recommendation and that the other be developed by an ad hoc committee of the board, with all board members invited to participate as interested. Or as a result of a workshop, a board might determine either to request the superintendent to bring forward during the following 6 months a major reform policy or determine that because of circumstances it would be better for the superintendent to appoint a task force of community leaders and district administrators to develop a recommendation for the superintendent to review and pass on to the board.

Everything depends on circumstances, such as the interest and knowledge of board members, the potential for controversy, other issues that might be demanding the attention of the superintendent, whether the state legislature is in session, or whether board elections are looming. Sometimes a superintendent might want the board out in front on a controversial policy, for example, outsourcing major business functions, variable and performance pay for teachers, bilingual education, or promotion standards for students. Sometimes the board might want the superintendent out in front. Every situation is unique.

Table 7.1 is a summary of these points, but it should not be read as prescriptive. The best political judgment of the board-superintendent team should determine, case by case, what method is preferred.

POLICY DEVELOPMENT PRINCIPLES

Three related principles apply to all policies, whether routine operating or reform, whether highly visible and controversial or almost unnoticed: Policies should focus on ends, not means; they should be only as specific as necessary to obtain results; and they should allow management as much freedom as possible.[1] Good policies are guides to action to achieve clearly defined results. They are more than goals, but they are most assuredly not operating manuals.

What board members want out of policies are results. So results should be described in as much detail as necessary to be clear about what is desired, but no more. Insufficient detail leaves ambiguity, and in effect requires no action. Too much specificity takes the board beyond its sphere of competence and limits management's ability to respond to changing circumstances.

Consider two examples; first, a routine operating policy. Because of the risks associated with allowing visitors access to schools, a superintendent

Table 7.1. Policy Development Matrix

	Noncontroversial Routine Operating Policies	*Noncontroversial Reform Policies*	*Controversial Operating Policies*	*Controversial Reform Policies*	*Policies Relating Only to Boards*
Number of policies per year	Many	Few	Few	Few	Few
Most likely policy development method	Superintendent recommends	Superintendent recommends	Superintendent charters task force	Superintendent charters task force	Board committee recommends
Alternative policy development method	Superintendent recommends	Board committee recommends	Superintendent recommends	Board committee recommends	Board charters task force

decides to recommend a policy requiring all school visitors to sign in and obtain a name badge. The agenda item prepared by the superintendent might include the rationale, the projected cost, and the relationship of this policy to other related policies. The agenda item, however, should not specify the method for posting the policy in schools, the sign-in book, and the badge. Not only would this be unnecessary; it would be foolish. However, a board policy stating only that the district should regulate the access of visitors to schools would require no action by management and be meaningless.

Next, consider a reform policy. Because of low math and science scores and input from local universities and employers, a board decides it wants to increase the number and quality of math and science credits required for high school graduation. An effective policy would not just state, "To meet graduation requirements students must take more math and science." Neither would it prescribe the exact curriculum down to the content of exit exams for each math or science course. What it would do is specify the number of math and science Carnegie units required, list the classes that would qualify for inclusion, and perhaps direct the superintendent to develop a standard curriculum and exit exam for each course for use throughout the district.

The agenda item, perhaps presented as a recommendation of the superintendent, might include information on math and science achievement by current students, changing college entrance requirements or job opportunities in the city, steps the district proposed to attract and provide professional development for math and science teachers, the cost and time required to build additional science labs in schools, anticipated changes in student schedules, the impact of the new requirement on high school electives, and total projected costs. This information would not be part of the policy. It would be included in the agenda item to explain to all interested parties why the board was acting and how the action would change high schools. Good policies educate as they direct.

Policies should focus on ends, not means. Does this indicate that policies should never mandate processes? No, for sometimes the essence of an issue is the process.

Consider pupil-assignment policies. A board might wish to establish a public school choice system that allows children to attend any elementary school in a high school feeder pattern or any high school in the district, provided space is available. The board might see this policy as a reform policy aligned with weighted student funding and other policies supporting a performance/empowerment theory of action.

Few issues are as contentious as pupil assignment. Given a choice, many parents will do almost anything to get their child in the "best" school. A pupil-assignment policy would be an excellent candidate for development by a task force of parents, principals, and administrators from transportation and finance and with strong representation from the city's ethnic communities.

A pupil-assignment policy would have to determine if some children (neighborhood children or siblings, for example) deserve preference, set guidelines for transportation, and establish processes to guarantee fairness and transparency. Specifically, the policy would need to ensure that parents had clear and accessible information about schools and fair and transparent processes for application, notification, lotteries at high-demand schools, deadlines, and appeals. In short, the policy would focus on standards and processes.

Yet it would be a mistake in this example or any policy dealing with process for a board to prescribe processes in too much detail. Detailed process requirements would limit management flexibility and provoke endless complaints and could be used to justify lawsuits. Just as results should be described in as much detail as necessary to obtain desired results, but no more, so processes should be described in as much detail as necessary to guarantee fairness and transparency, but no more.

The fundamental fact about organizations that underlie these policy development principles is that the only people who really know the details of any job are those who do the work. And even if policy makers at a point in time knew exactly what needed to be done, circumstances might change. What worked today might not work tomorrow.

Boards must keep in mind that management is accomplishing predetermined work through others. Boards, with the help of their superintendent, get to decide what the work is, but superintendents, acting through a management system of delegation and controls, must determine how the work is to be done. So policies, which set standards and provide guides and constraints to action, should focus on desired results, deal with processes only when absolutely necessary, provide enough clarity so that management knows exactly what the board intends, and grant management as much flexibility as possible to fill in the gaps and make changes as circumstances require.

POLICY OVERSIGHT

The board's responsibility for policy does not end with policy approval. Management oversight, a board responsibility, includes more than oversight of business operations. It also includes oversight of policy implementation and evaluation of policy effectiveness. Boards need to know if the policies they have approved are being effectively implemented and if they are achieving the desired results.

Boards cannot assume that policies will be effectively implemented. Reform policies, especially, are likely to generate significant internal resistance. Rick Hess points out:

> This is not due to personnel failings or ill intentions but because teachers and administrators have entered a system and grown accustomed to one set of rules. Reform boards, almost by definition, are seeking to change those rules. They are typically telling personnel to do things differently, to learn new routines, to assume more responsibilities, and to tackle new challenges. Nowhere would we expect employees to enthusiastically embrace such change. (Personal communication, December 21, 2004)

To make certain that policies are properly and effectively implemented and strengthen the superintendent's hand in managing resistance, boards should make explicit how implementation will be measured and reported. The superintendent might be directed, for example, to report annually on action steps taken, systems established, and implementation milestones. Few boards would have difficulty listing evidence they would like to see to demonstrate successful implementation of increased math and science requirements for high school graduation or public school choice.

Implementation is not enough. Policies must work. Sometimes policies, however well implemented, do not achieve desired results. All major operating and reform policies must be periodically evaluated. Are the new policies saving money; improving teacher recruitment; giving principals more control over budgets and personnel; improving student attendance, discipline, or achievement? How are the new policies aligned with other policies? Are there unintended consequences? Just as the board makes explicit how implementation will be measured and reported, it should make explicit how and when major policies will be evaluated for results.

The most effective method for policy oversight is for the board to place in the policy document a statement describing how and when the superintendent will report on implementation and results. Preparing this statement requires close collaboration with the superintendent, for the superintendent's knowledge of public education and the district makes him or her the prime source on how to measure policy implementation and effectiveness.

Once this statement has been agreed upon, placed in the policy, and formally approved by the board, the board, assured that it will receive the information it wants at the appointed time, can turn its attention to other matters and not bother the superintendent with repeated requests for information. And the superintendent, free from time-consuming questions and second-guessing by board members about implementation steps or effectiveness, can manage with clarity, knowing exactly what is expected and when. In addition, when he or she faces internal resistance to change—which with reform policies is the rule rather than the exception—the superintendent can make clear to the staff that he or she has no choice: The board is expecting a specific report on a date certain, and it must be done.

When boards and superintendents, building on positive relationships and effective governance processes, understand the place of policy in their work and the power of reform policies, and when they collaboratively develop policies using the methods and principles outlined in this chapter, they have in their hands a powerful set of levers for transforming school districts.

CHAPTER 8

Policies to Transform Urban Districts

IN THE REFORM GOVERNANCE FRAMEWORK, the top box in the vertical column represents policy content (Figure 8.1). This is where all the previously described elements of reform governance come together. All the work of reform governance points to this objective: the right combination of aligned reform policies properly implemented. Even the work described in Chapter 9, Building Civic Capacity and Transition Planning, feeds back into the loop of core beliefs and theories of action to support reform policies.

Policies set standards and provide for the establishment of structures and processes. Just as good laws and the proper enforcement of these laws create the standards, structures, and processes that are the basis for civil society, so school district policies properly implemented create the standards, structures, and processes that are the basis of a working school district. Of course, there is more to an organization than standards, structures, and processes. Harmony and productivity in both civil society and school districts require that the laws or policies be written in the hearts of the people. Culture matters.

In both civil society and school districts, changing laws is difficult. Changing culture takes time. Changes in both start with leadership. In civil society, leaders, exercising the power of governance, legislate standards, structures, and processes, which change behaviors and over time change attitudes and values.

For a school district, leadership starts with the board. Through policy, the board sets standards and provides for the establishment of structures and processes. Culture follows structure and process. Structure and process can be changed; so, in time, can culture.

As mentioned above, policies can be routine operating policies or reform policies, controversial or almost unnoticed. Reform boards spend as little time as possible on routine operating policies, though on occasion such policies can be controversial and require considerable attention. Their focus is on major reform policies. These are the policies that can transform urban districts. As a rule, these policies are controversial, and developing them takes time. But reform boards do not resent the time this demands. Reform is their passion.

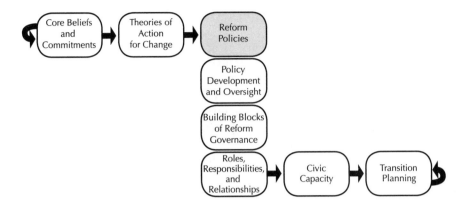

Figure 8.1. Reform policies as element of Reform Governance Framework.

Reform policies rest on a foundation of clear roles, positive relationships, effective governance processes, and board-superintendent partnership in policy development. They spring from the board's core beliefs and commitments, are driven by the board's theory of action for change, and are strategically aligned to support whole-systems change. Reform policies are the primary work product of reform boards. They stand at the apex of the Reform Governance Framework.

As Gail Littlejohn states:

Developing effective reform policies is hard work. It takes significant time, mental energy, and sometimes, emotional resilience. When done well, this work can transform an urban district. Reform policies set direction and drive high performance. They make possible immediate improvements and build for long-term solutions. Reforming an urban district takes many years. Aligned reform policies are the tool of choice for creating and sustaining change. (Personal communication, February 2, 2005)

What follows in this chapter is not an attempt to examine every possible reform policy. No one could claim knowledge of an inclusive list of reform policies. Nor is this chapter intended to delve deeply into a small sample of reform policies. Major reform policies are complex. Complete examination of even a few would require a book as long as this one. What I do in this chapter is outline the core reform policies and related issues that support the comprehensive theories of action that are currently gaining traction in urban districts.

POLICY FRAMEWORK FOR PERFORMANCE/EMPOWERMENT

As stated in Chapter 4, this theory of action focuses on results. Student achievement and performance of all district functions are measured in numerous and sophisticated ways, and there are positive and negative consequences for administrators, teachers, and students for meeting performance standards. Since employees are accountable, they must also be empowered. Participative management and employee involvement prevail, and as much power as possible is pushed out into schools and classrooms. Since students are accountable, parents, on their behalf, are also empowered. They are given public school choice and great influence in the schools they choose.

Standards

Performance/empowerment must begin with standards, such as academic content and performance standards, business process standards, safety standards, ethical standards, and parent and community satisfaction standards. Most of these standards already exist. They are defined in state education policy; state and federal law; city fire, safety, and building codes; and financial and accounting standards. Boards should know in general terms what these standards require and make certain that management has absolute mastery of them.

Where additional standards are required, for example, codes of student conduct, employee evaluations, and parent and community satisfaction, boards should ask management to bring forward policy recommendations. Specifically, boards should consider expanding academic standards beyond state requirements—promotion standards at Grades 3, 5, and 8, for example, or end-of-course examinations for core high school courses. Or a board could determine that every high school graduate should meet a certain standard of fluency in a second language.

All major district standards should be embedded in board policy.

Accountability

Accountability is holding people responsible for meeting standards. Without accountability, standards are not really standards, they are just goals. Accountability in public education is a surrogate for Adam Smith's invisible hand. In efficient markets, what enriches the producer also benefits the consumer. Self-interest is important. No system can depend on altruism alone. Accountability aligns the interests of the adults in the system with the interests of the children. Both benefit when the children learn.

Performance/empowerment requires accountability systems. District accountability systems identify important performance indicators, measure performance using these indicators, collect and distribute performance data, and apply predetermined consequences (rankings, rewards, sanctions, interventions, or a combination of these) to schools and functional work units for achieving predefined outcomes. Outcome measures are more important than process measures, but process measures are important, for they predict outcomes. Normally, outcome measures are part of the accountability system established by the board, and process measures are part of management's infrastructure for supporting school improvement.

District accountability systems go beyond the requirements of state accountability systems and NCLB. State systems and NCLB apply equally to all and paint with a broad brush. District systems are tailored to the needs of the district, measure performance in multiple and sophisticated ways, and are continuously improved.

For example, a district may want to use two assessments to measure student performance, perhaps a criterion-referenced test (CRT) and a norm-referenced test (NRT). It may wish to set a higher standard than the state standard for acceptable performance or demand greater improvements from year to year. It may wish to establish multiple cut-points in assessments in order to measure performance at multiple levels, for example, basic, proficient, and advanced, or it may wish to measure performance using scale scores and very sophisticated statistical analyses of performance curves. It may wish to assess performance in additional areas at additional grade levels.

A district may wish to develop end-of-course examinations to assess high school performance, or hold high schools accountable for the percentage of students taking advanced courses. It may wish to measure graduation rates in different ways; and almost certainly a district will want to measure school safety, parent and community satisfaction, and other indicators of school performance.

Flexibility is another advantage of a district accountability system. Unlike federal or state policy makers, school boards can more easily fine-tune or expand their systems to close loopholes, raise standards, measure achievement with additional assessments, change weights for accountability measures, or in other ways continuously improve their systems.

Accountability implies consequences, both positive and negative. Without consequences, there is no accountability. One does not measure just to obtain information. One measures to change behavior.

The public spotlight is the first and most effective consequence. Bold newspaper headlines, Web postings, newsletters to parents, and signs in front of schools proclaiming them exemplary or recognized motivate teachers, principals, and other district employees. Moreover, the spotlight will likely bring forth praise or demands for improvement from parents.

In addition to the spotlight, districts have at their disposal a wide range of responses to high or low performance. High performance can be rewarded with additional flexibility in school management, additional resources, or group awards or bonuses to school employees. Negative responses can include performance audits, mandated school-improvement plans, district assistance, intervention teams, employee transfers, and partial or full reconstitution.

What applies to schools also applies to other functional units of the district. Transportation, security, facilities management, food service, and Central Office functions can be rewarded or disciplined for their success or failure to meet predetermined performance goals designed to enhance their service to schools.

Designing and implementing a district accountability system is not easy. There are scores of complex issues to consider.[1] It will take a district several years to implement and fine-tune an effective district system. But boards have few levers for change more powerful than a district accountability system. What is measured is what gets done. What boards value they should measure.

The performance/empowerment theory of action requires not just school and functional-unit accountability. It also requires individual accountability. This means that boards must reexamine district human-resource management systems. Few issues in public education are more controversial than teacher job security and compensation. In the prevailing 20th-century district design, teachers and other district employees have significant job security and are held accountable for compliance and rewarded for years of service. Performance/empowerment holds employees accountable for results, though some compliance is always necessary, and rewards high performance.

In a performance culture, student performance at the school and classroom levels is reflected in principal and teacher evaluations and has some impact on compensation. Given the single-salary schedule in most state education codes and union contracts, this is difficult to achieve. Boards committed to accountability must push for change as the political environment permits. In the long run, a performance culture is incompatible with a salary schedule that rewards administrators and teachers just for time behind the desk or in front of the class.

To the extent possible, districts need to be able to assign principals to the schools that need them most or move them to nonleadership positions or out of the system if they cannot perform. The same is true of teachers. Principals must be able to build a team that best meets the needs of the school. There is no place in an accountability culture for principal or teacher job placement by seniority.

What is true for principals and teachers is also true for regional and Central Office administrators. In fact, every job in a performance-driven school district should be tied to performance indicators and every school district employee should be subject to similar positive or negative consequences for performance. An effective district accountability system inevitably leads to major changes in human resource management policies.

Performance/empowerment also requires students to be accountable. This means promotion and graduation standards. This is really nothing new. There have always been promotion and graduation standards: Teachers determined whether a child was performing on grade level or had passed a course. The difference in a performance/empowerment system is that the district includes standardized assessments in the standards for promotion or graduation, and instead of simply making a child repeat a grade or course puts into place effective alternatives for children who do not meet promotion standards.

Empowerment

So far, the focus has been on accountability, but performance/empowerment requires accountability *and* empowerment. Principals and teachers cannot fairly be held accountable for student achievement if they do not have significant control over their work. It is a management axiom as old as civilization: Responsibility and authority go together. Within the word *empowerment* are lumped together all the policies, systems, and practices that enable principals, teachers, and others in the system to control, to as large a degree as possible, the environment in which they do their work.

This principle has been recognized since the late 1980s, when school-based shared decision-making committees (SDMCs) became popular. Miami-Dade County (Florida) received much attention for placing SDMCs in a large percentage of its schools. In 1988, the Illinois legislature required the Chicago Public Schools district to establish elected school committees with the authority to hire and fire principals. By the mid-1990s, a large number of states were requiring the establishment of SDMCs, usually mandating that teachers comprise a majority of the committees. Site-based management was all the rage in school reform.

Site-based management, however, is incompatible with performance/empowerment, for the emphasis of site-based management is on empowerment without balancing accountability. Districts can hold principals accountable for results. They cannot hold committees of teachers, parents, and community representatives accountable. Throughout the 1990s, as state accountability systems placed increasing performance pressure on schools, the power of SDMCs faded.

This was certainly the case in Houston, where a researcher pointed out the fading of SDMC power and concluded that "there is a contradiction between further empowering SDMCs and holding principals accountable that will be difficult to resolve" (Leal, 2000, p. 14).

San Diego's experience, as described by Ron Ottinger, was not atypical:

San Diego was one of the first large urban school districts to buy into the site-based management theory of action. Prodded by the teachers union, school management councils were created with a requirement that at least 50% plus one of the members be teachers. Principals, like all other members, had just one vote. At the same time, the teachers union refused to agree to a district accountability system to hold schools accountable for student achievement.

The result was a balkanization of the system: the proliferation and widespread diffusion of curriculum, instruction, and professional development programs. In 1996, the union struck the district around the rallying cry of teacher involvement, and won, cementing the failed site-based management policy and ensuring that teachers would continue as independent contractors who could close their classroom doors and be accountable to no one. Principals became almost powerless.

When Alan Bersin became superintendent, he and Tony Alvarado were convinced that the old system of site-based management was so ingrained in the San Diego culture that it literally needed to be blown up. Only by abolishing the system entirely could they put into place a new system that placed instruction and the ongoing training and support of teachers, with accountability for results, at the heart of San Diego's reforms. (Personal communication, December 21, 2004)

One major constellation of policies that maximizes the empowerment of principals and parents and also fosters equity is weighted student funding. It replaces program and staff-based budgeting with student-based budgeting. But it is more than a budgeting change. It is the creation of an entirely new budget/school-management system that unleashes powerful marketplace forces within the district. Combined with accountability and public school choice, weighted student funding can transform a district's culture.[2]

Joseph Olchefske, who as chief financial officer and superintendent implemented weighted student funding in Seattle, concurs:

I believe that a dramatic, systemwide change to a district's funding system, like weighted student funding, will have a catalytic effect on a district's overall reform strategy. By its very nature, a change of this magnitude in the funding of schools touches virtually every corner of the district's operations and sends an incredibly powerful message to the workforce and the community about the seriousness of the board's commitment to the reform agenda. (Personal communication, December 20, 2004)

In the prevailing 20th-century district model, resources are allocated to schools based on complex formulas that take into consideration numbers, levels, and types of students, but the major determinant is staffing needs. Based on student population and school programs (placed at schools per board policy), Central Office, following staffing-pattern guidelines, determines how many staff positions will be allocated to each school. Then, calculating average salaries for teachers and other school-based employees, and adding formula-driven amounts for materials, supplies, and other items, Central Office sets the budgets for schools.

Services provided to schools by Central Office, for example, special education or curriculum supervisors, are provided free. These costs are charged to Central Office, as are costs for utilities, maintenance, custodial services, grounds, and so on. Because budget control rests in Central Office, an elementary school principal with a school budget of $2 million will likely control no more than $80,000 or so in special-purpose funds.

Weighted student funding turns this system on its head. It funds children directly rather than indirectly through those who serve them. Each child is assigned dollars, weighted to account for the cost of his or her education. Children with no special needs receive a standard weight of 1. Children with special needs, for example, at-risk children or English-language learners, receive an additional weight, perhaps 1.2 or 1.15. The board can also assign added weights to high-cost grade levels, for example, assigning higher weights to K–2 children to fund smaller classes or to high school students to fund elective courses or additional counselors.

Money follows the child. School budgets are based on average daily attendance (or enrollment) of weighted students. Larger schools with more high-cost students receive more money. Districts can also require schools to accept responsibility for minor maintenance, custodial, and grounds and budget funds for these purposes based on the size, age, and condition of school buildings.

Schools are charged for staff based on actual salary and benefit costs or on average costs for various classifications of employees. Actual salaries are preferred, because average salaries cause schools that are filled primarily with poor children to subsidize schools filled primarily with middle-class children. The poor school is charged the average salary for each teacher, even though a majority of teachers are likely to be less experienced and lower paid. And the middle-class school is charged for the average salary for each teacher, even though a majority of the teachers are likely to be more experienced and higher paid.

Principals are free to purchase goods or services from within or without the district (most likely limited to a certified list of vendors that have been prequalified by the district for quality and price). And principals are allowed to carry over gains or losses from one year to the next.

Weighted student funding links resource-allocation decisions directly with the needs of children. Principals, under great pressure to produce high achievement, are free to configure their workforces to meet the needs of their students. They can have fewer high-paid master teachers and larger classes, or smaller classes taught by a larger workforce of lower-paid teachers, or a mix of the two. They can put more of their resources into instruction, or if their students benefit more from the services of counselors, social workers, and nurses, shift resources to professional support staff. And they can shift resources fairly quickly to respond to changing priorities.

By giving principals the authority to allocate resources and carry over gains and losses, weighted student funding promotes improved district services to schools. District services that are not competitive with outside vendors, whether professional services or services for minor maintenance repairs, either improve value or go out of business.

The full value of weighted student funding is not achieved unless parents are given public school choice and principals the authority, within reasonable limits, to pay teachers for performance and dismiss low performers.

Public school choice encourages schools to compete for students, particularly those who bring with them the most money. Schools have an incentive to offer the programs and services parents want, provide high-quality instruction, and keep parents happy. Like private schools, they are in a competitive market. But unlike private schools, they have an incentive to compete for poor children rather than rich ones. The leadership of schools that don't compete can be replaced. Parents exercise their customer power not primarily by influencing what happens in the school their child attends, but rather by taking their child and the money attached to him or her to the school of their choice. The school district becomes a regulated, internal marketplace.

Weighted student funding, balanced with public school choice and school-based personnel management, has powerful consequences: It guarantees equity. *Equity* in public education should be defined as "unequal resources for unequal needs." With weighted student funding, children with greater needs receive more money.

It is almost impossible with traditional program and staff budgeting to guarantee equity. Districts that examine themselves for equity invariably discover that children with the same needs receive significantly different amounts of real dollars per year depending on the schools they attend. In an analysis of district funding inequities, researchers found that schools within the same district can receive wildly different real-dollar allocations, and often it is high-poverty, low-performing schools that lose out (Roza & Hawley Miles, 2002a).

Weighted student funding is complex, but its goals are simple: guarantee equity; empower principals to manage for results; push the maximum possible percentage of district money to schools; link resources closely with results; increase productivity; and empower parents by giving them choice with real consequences for the schools they choose, or fail to choose. And once in place, weighted student funding systems make it easy for boards to monitor resource allocation, link resources to results, and quickly move resources to reflect priorities by changing weights.

Capacity

Accountability and empowerment policies require significant investments in systems, technology, training, research, and evaluation. Many job responsibilities change. New jobs, even new departments, are created. Administrators, especially principals and school business managers, need training. Enterprise resource systems are needed for complex financial, human resource, and student information-management systems. Standards, measures, tracking systems, data integrity, evaluations, and much more are required. Change is not inexpensive.

Performance/Empowerment Policies

Following is a summary of the major policy issues for performance/empowerment, described above. Each might require board approval of several specific aligned policies, implemented over time, to establish a comprehensive policy framework. A fully developed performance/empowerment district would require scores of specific policies, all developed with great care, all aligned, and all carefully staged to build on what had gone before and prepare the way for what the board intended for the future.

- Ensure that systems are in place for knowing and enforcing all federal, state, and local laws, codes, and standards.
- Approve additional district standards: curriculum, end-of-course examinations, promotion, graduation, business practices, ethics, codes, and so on.
- Approve additional district assessments of academic achievement.
- Approve performance indicators, measures, and rating systems.
- Approve consequences: recognition, rewards, and interventions for schools.
- Establish the powers of school SDMCs, where they exist.
- Establish student weights for weighted student funding.
- Consider issues, such as small-school subsidies, that might be required to maintain equity for weighted student funding.
- Determine charges to schools for staff (actual or average salaries) and district services.
- Approve annually lists of certified vendors available to principals for the purchase of goods and services.

- Review the decision-making authority of principals.
- Approve human resource policies regarding teacher recruiting, vetting, contracts, salary schedule, other compensation issues, evaluations, recognitions, rewards, and transfers.
- Approve policies regarding financial controls, school and other internal audits, and guidelines for the year-to-year carryover of school gains and losses.
- Approve guidelines to regulate public school choice, including choice zones (if any), transportation policies, preferences (neighborhood children, siblings, special education, etc.), appeals, and so forth.

POLICY FRAMEWORK FOR MANAGED INSTRUCTION

This theory of action is based on the belief that to significantly improve student achievement, districts must directly manage instruction. Building on academic content and performance standards, districts construct a curriculum that covers every subject for every grade in elementary and middle school and every course in high school. The curriculum is coherent, aligned, and detailed down to individual lesson plans, required teaching materials, and sample assessments. Professional development is about the curriculum and how to teach it. Teaching is continually monitored. Formative assessments are frequent. And a comprehensive student information-management system tracks student performance. Everything about instruction that can be managed is managed.

District Web Sites

In recent years, a growing number of districts have become well versed in the knowledge and practice of managed instruction. As mentioned earlier, many of the highest-performing urban districts in the nation have reasonably effective managed-instruction systems in place. Clear outlines of managed instruction can be found on the Web sites of many of the districts that have acted on this theory of action.

Council of the Great City Schools

Another guide for the implementation of managed instruction are the reports of the Strategic Support Teams of the Council of the Great City Schools. These teams of professionals from other districts are assembled by the council to provide technical assistance to member districts. The reports are more than audits and recommendations on instructional practice; they assess the full range of district operations, including governance. But at their core are extensive recommendations on instructional management. These sections are gold mines. They are almost exhaustive lists of recommendations outlining the steps needed to implement comprehensive instructional-management systems.

The report to the District of Columbia Public Schools, for example, contains 107 recommendations, all but 2 or 3 directly focused on the creation of an instructional-management system. Although the report responds to conditions in Washington, DC, the recommendations provide a comprehensive checklist that every urban district would be wise to review. The same is true for reports on Buffalo, Detroit, Dayton, and others, all currently available from the council (Council of the Great City Schools, 2004).

National Center for Educational Accountability

However, the most balanced summary of managed instruction and perhaps the most useful place to begin is the National Center for Educational Accountability (NCEA) Web site (*www.nc4ea.org*). NCEA is a collaborative effort of the Education Commission of the States, the University of Texas at Austin, and Just for the Kids. Its mission is to "improve learning through the effective use of school and student data and the identification of best practices." On the Web site are outlines of best instructional practices in urban districts that were finalists for the Broad Prize for Urban Education.

The NCEA Web site identifies five best-practices areas, provides a list of best practices in each area, and for each best practice provides a Web link to a district Web site for a detailed description of the practice. Under each best-practice area is a short essay describing what the practice involves. The knowledge base available to district policy makers and executives is enormous. This summary of district best practices will be updated annually and likely become the bible for managed instruction (NCEA, n.d.).

The five best-practice areas are the following:

- Define clear and specific academic objectives by grade and subject.
- Provide strong instructional leaders, highly qualified teachers, and aligned professional development.
- Provide evidence-based instructional programs.
- Develop student assessment and data-monitoring systems to monitor school performance.
- Recognize, intervene, or adjust based on school performance.

Below, taken directly from the NCEA Web site, are the specific best practices listed in each best-practice area:

Define clear and specific academic objectives by grade and subject.

- Academic objectives for each grade level and/or subject area delineate the specific things that teachers are to teach and students are to learn.
- Clearly written curricular documents exist at the district level for K–12 subject areas.
- The district provides support materials to help schools understand and teach specific curriculum objectives.
- The specific knowledge and skills to be gained by grade and subject are deeply understood and integrated throughout the school system.

Provide strong instructional leaders, highly qualified teachers, and aligned professional development.

- A clear process identifies and develops internal candidates for instructional leadership positions.
- A powerful induction program supports teachers and leaders new to the district.
- Comprehensive programs to support teachers are present.
- Hiring teachers that fit the needs of individual schools is a high priority.
- Principal professional development centers on curriculum and instruction.
- Principal professional development is targeted to needs that are identified from school performance data.
- Professional development for teachers is directly related to teaching and provides opportunities for practice in the classroom.
- The principal selection process examines the candidate's record of raising student achievement with similar populations.

Provide evidence-based instructional programs.

- A clear process for the review and selection of district instructional programs requires evidence of the program's effectiveness in other schools with similar student populations.
- A rubric or chart shows the connection between academic objectives and selected instructional programs at all school levels. The rubric specifies pages or activities from the instructional program aligned to the actual academic objective.
- Before final adoption of recommended instructional programs, the district pilots those programs in its schools.
- Scientifically based instructional programs are in place.
- Scientifically based instructional programs are non-negotiable in terms of use in every classroom.
- The district mandates that specific scientifically based instructional programs are used in every classroom.

Develop student assessment and data monitoring systems to monitor school performance.

- A district data system with unique student identifiers makes it possible to collect, store, disaggregate, and distribute student performance data.
- At the beginning of the school year, the district provides the teachers a standard set of reports on the performance of students they will teach in the coming year.
- District personnel regularly visit schools to examine teaching and learning processes.
- Student performance reports are disaggregated by numerous factors.
- Teachers and principals can obtain supplementary customized student performance reports from the district.
- The district data system can be accessed by principals and all teachers.
- The district data system stores information on many student performance indicators.
- The district data system tracks student information longitudinally.
- The district has a clear process for establishing goals. The district uses data regularly to evaluate its success in achieving the goals, and adjusts practices accordingly.
- The district provides benchmark assessments in all core academic areas to monitor performance throughout the year, typically at two or three designated checkpoints.
- The district regularly evaluates the effectiveness of school-level personnel.

Recognize, intervene, or adjust based on school performance.

- In order to assess the effectiveness of their programs and to determine future interventions, the district tracks a history of interventions for each student performing below grade level.
- Increases in principal pay are linked to student performance outcomes.
- Intervention strategies with students performing below grade level are continually evaluated for effectiveness.
- Monetary incentives and other rewards such as public recognition encourage schools to reach their student performance goals.
- Students performing below grade level are provided with intensive intervention until they reach grade level.
- Students performing below grade level begin intervention programs prior to the first year of state testing.
- The district focuses resources on schools that are not reaching student performance goals.
- The district has a well-defined series of successively more targeted programs to assist students not responding to initial interventions.
- The district holds schools accountable for the performance of their students. (NCEA, n.d.)

Policies for Managed Instruction

As is clear from this brief outline of managed instruction, most of the work that needs to be done is management work. And indeed, throughout urban America, the leadership for managed instruction has come from superintendents, supported by chief academic officers and other professional staff.

Managed instruction does not require as much policy leadership from boards as does performance/empowerment. However, where superintendents have successfully implemented managed instruction, boards have provided essential support. They have made clear to all that student achievement is their priority; they have approved policies and provided resources as needed, and they have sometimes had to stand with their superintendents in the face of fierce resistance to change.

Managed instruction should start with a clear declaration of intent, plan of action, or blueprint approved by the board. The board must understand clearly the magnitude of the changes that are proposed and be committed to providing policy and financial support through thick and thin, for resistance is likely. In addition, the board must develop and support a communication plan designed to enlist the workforce, parents, community leaders, and active citizens.

Specific policy issues for managed instruction include a few of the same policies required for performance/empowerment, but also encompass many new ones and require a board to devote considerable attention to budgets, for managed instruction requires significant capacity building:

- Approve district standards, for curriculum, end-of-course examinations, promotion, graduation, and so forth.
- Approve additional district assessments of academic achievement.
- Approve performance indicators, measures, and rating systems.
- Approve policies for staff selection, promotion, and transfer.
- Approve professional development standards, requirements, and programs.
- Approve partnerships with universities regarding teacher education programs.
- Fund development of a comprehensive, aligned curriculum.
- Fund research-based instructional materials.
- Approve contracts with vendors for instructional materials and support services, for example, reading programs.
- Approve and fund professional development programs for principals and teachers.
- Approve and fund school-based coaches in literacy, math, science, and other subjects.

- Establish research and evaluation departments for selecting instructional materials and evaluating performance at all levels.
- Approve and fund comprehensive student information-management systems.

POLICY FRAMEWORK FOR MANAGED PERFORMANCE/EMPOWERMENT

As stated in Chapter 4, both performance/empowerment and managed instruction are incomplete as theories of action. Both miss something important. Managed instruction does not create incentives for the adults in the system, does not stimulate innovation, does not build stakeholders, and does not create a performance culture. It is compliance based.

Performance/empowerment, by combining accountability for results with empowerment, aligns adult incentives with student achievement. It creates stakeholders within the organization for the new system, promotes innovation, and gradually transforms a compliance culture into a performance culture. Performance/empowerment, however, fails to meet the needs of highly mobile urban children and neglects process improvement of the instructional system. It makes no effort to manage the district's core business.

Blending managed instruction with performance/empowerment to create a managed-performance/empowerment district requires bringing together the policy frameworks outlined above. With the exception of Gwinnett County, the few districts that have done this started with one theory of action and then gradually blended in the other.

The key to this blend is flexibility. In a managed-instruction or performance/empowerment district, policies generally apply to all schools. In a managed-performance/empowerment district, wide ranges of reform policies apply to individual schools based on circumstances.

Note how Boston superintendent Payzant, describing steps taken to blend performance/empowerment with a mature instructional-management system, captures this point: "Giving more flexibility in Boston to schools with better performance has created incentives for all of our schools, while allowing central administrators to concentrate more on the schools that need the most help" (personal communication, January 3, 2005).

Creating a managed-performance/empowerment system rests on three major insights about urban district design: Student achievement at high levels is impossible without an instructional-management system as well as district standards, accountability, and empowerment; these two major theories of action for transforming urban districts are not incompatible; and all schools do not need to be treated the same and, in fact, perform better if they are not. Once a board-superintendent team arrives at these conclusions it can, with patience and care, create a managed-performance/empowerment system.

Consider how this might work. In Figure 8.2, Policy Framework for Managed Performance/Empowerment, the dark portion in the middle represents tightly coupled district management of the school's instructional core. In a managed-performance/empowerment system, board policy can specify that more or less of the curriculum be managed depending on grade level, performance level, or some other variable. That is, the inner box can be larger or smaller. Likewise, board policy can specify that the curriculum that is managed can be so within narrow or wide parameters. That is, the inner box can be shaded more lightly or more darkly. In other words, core subjects in elementary and middle school and core high school classes are more likely to be tightly coupled than noncore subjects or classes, and higher-performing schools are likely to be given greater control over teaching materials, professional development, coaching, and monitoring in these core subjects and classes.

The same flexibility can be given to school operations. Depending on performance in the operational area, schools can be given more or less control of budgets, personnel, procurement, and schedules. All principals do not need to be treated the same. A district need not limit the operational free-

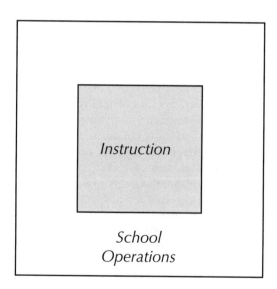

Figure 8.2. Policy framework for managed performance/empowerment. Shaded area indicates tightly coupled district management, with compliance-based accountability. White area indicates loosely coupled district management, with performance-based accountability.

dom of principals willing and able to manage school operations as business centers, but it would be foolish to empower principals not yet ready to accept this responsibility.

POLICY FRAMEWORK FOR CHARTER DISTRICTS

A fourth comprehensive theory of action available to urban boards is charter districts. Charter districts do not operate schools; rather, they manage a portfolio of charter schools. The district does not employ principals, teachers, and other school staff; they are employees of the organizations that hold the charters. The district may own all the school buildings, or the facilities may be owned in any combination by the district, a real estate trust set up by the district, or charter operators.

The Education Commission of the States (1999) report *Governing America's Schools: Changing the Rules* is the foundation document for charter districts (see also Hill, 2001; Rotherham, 2001). It describes the characteristics of what it calls "a system of publicly authorized, publicly funded and independently operated schools" and outlines specific state, district, and school responsibilities. Specifically, the district has the responsibility to do the following:

- Survey community leaders, employers, parents, and students to determine needs.
- Issue requests for proposals to open schools that serve these needs.
- Consider unsolicited proposals for schools that demonstrate sufficient community interest.
- Analyze the need for new types of schools and identify promising potential school operators.
- Establish general criteria for approving proposals.
- Create fair proposal-review processes open to all qualified school operators.
- Establish standards to exclude schools run by either hate groups or religious organizations that do not adhere to applicable U.S. Supreme Court doctrines governing the separation of church and state.
- Operate schools when there is a community need that others are unable or unwilling to meet.
- Establish weighted student-funding formulas to guarantee equity and attract the interest of charter operators to operate schools for special needs children.
- Approve charters, which detail goals, pedagogy, target population, student admissions and disciplinary criteria, funding, and freedoms and constraints on personnel.

- Work with superintendent to negotiate, review, and renew charters.
- Monitor performance of schools against district standards, including attendance; dropouts; truancy; disciplinary problems; turnover rates of faculty; status of graduates; student-portfolio assessments; qualitative school reviews; and surveys of parents, students, and employers.
- Provide, if necessary, special incentives to charter operators to operate in low-income areas or serve primarily disadvantaged children.
- Contract with independent-analysis organizations to conduct periodic reviews of school quality.
- Provide mechanisms for immediate interventions or temporary management of schools that violate charters in significant ways.
- Establish communication systems for continual reporting to parents and citizens regarding the performance of schools.
- Ensuring sufficient supply of schools so that dissatisfied parents can quickly transfer children to other schools.

The policy work by a board to design a charter district would be extensive, but the most difficult challenge would be the transition from the status quo to charter district. The smoothest transition would be from a fully developed performance/empowerment district to a charter district. An accountability system and significant empowerment, including weighted student funding, would already be in place. The most difficult transition issues would be transferring teachers and other district employees from district employment to charter school employment and resolving issues regarding facilities. Some transitions would require changes in state law. But in most states, boards interested in creating charter districts have the authority to move a long way down this path.

REFORM GOVERNANCE POLICY LEADERSHIP

Whether performance/empowerment, managed instruction, managed performance/empowerment, charter districts, or a mixed portfolio of these, the changes required to redesign urban districts are so large that superintendents alone cannot do what needs to be done. Major redesigns of urban districts require extensive leadership by the board of education.

Managed instruction, because it builds most closely on the 20th-century model—simply adding instruction to everything else the district manages—requires less board leadership than do the other redesigns. Policy and budget work, however, is significant, and political cover for the superintendent can be a major challenge. Reallocation of resources, requirements for professional development, frequent observations of classroom practice, and teacher evaluations linked to student achievement may be perceived as threats to teacher independence and stimulate fierce resistance. Boards acting on a managed-instruction theory of action must be involved, committed, and clearly identified as mandating change.

The leadership and policy work to redesign districts on the balanced principles of performance and empowerment is huge and guaranteed to be controversial. Accountability, because it shines the spotlight on low performance and responds with consequences, threatens school communities, principals, teachers, and others. Teacher unions and other employee groups will vigorously oppose changes in human resource policies that decrease job security and increase rewards for performance. The single salary schedule is almost sacred to teacher unions. Weighted student funding, because it will transfer resources from schools in middle-class neighborhoods to schools in poor neighborhoods, will likely upset residents of middle-class neighborhoods, and public school choice supported by reasonable transportation policies will further upset those in middle-class neighborhoods by bringing more poor children into middle-class schools.

Performance/empowerment transforms jobs, systems, and culture. It requires extensive board knowledge of reform theory and practice, organizational dynamics, and whole-systems change. And it requires political savvy and nerves of steel. This goes doubly for the challenge of bringing managed instruction and performance/empowerment together into managed performance/empowerment.

Charter district redesign is a revolution. The policy work is enormous. But the real barrier is politics. Charter districts cannot be created without broad public support. Board leaders committed to charter districts will need to build powerful political bases and extensive alliances with major power centers in their cities and states, and they will need a superintendent who has an extraordinary talent for politics, leadership, design work, and management.

Whatever theory of action and aligned policy framework a board pursues, the work is time consuming, controversial, and politically risky. Board members, however, should not be deterred by controversy. As Joseph Olchefske points out:

> Any major reform of a school district is by its very nature controversial. The fundamental objective of reform is to upset the status quo, and there are powerful groups whose interests are well served by the status quo. A reform board will hear howls of protest from those whose applecart is upset by the change. Unfortunately, they will hear little from those who see the long-term positive impact of the change. But these people are out there, waiting to be mobilized for support. Boards must have faith in this broad support for

change and work to bring it to the table. (Personal communication, December 20, 2004)

Reform leadership is controversial, sometimes even painful, but it is also creative, stimulating, and rewarding. It is the board's work. But it is not work the board can do by itself; to borrow from the title of a book by Hill, Campbell, and Harvey (2000), it takes a city. And as Olchefske affirms, the city is out there waiting to be led.

CHAPTER 9

Building Civic Capacity and Transition Planning

REFORM GOVERNANCE MEANS MORE THAN the practice of good governance and policy leadership for change. It also means leading the community to support change and planning for the future. Schools are rooted deeply in the communities they serve. The public owns them and directly or indirectly chooses those who govern them. The public must support change and continue to choose reform leaders to lead change.

The Reform Governance Framework shows two boxes extending to the right of Roles, Responsibilities, and Relationships, the foundation box that supports everything the board does (see Figure 9.1). The first box, Civic Capacity, represents the work of the board in the community to build support for the board's core beliefs and commitments, theory of action, and aligned reform policies. The second box, Transition Planning, represents the board's planning for change so that successive board-superintendent teams follow the same reform path.

Building civic capacity is crucial. Everyone is for better schools, but change frightens many special interests, especially employee groups and, sometimes, middle-class parents. A board-superintendent team that gets too far in front of the public it serves will find itself without support. And without broad public support, special interest groups will kill bold reform policies.

Moreover, broad public support for the board's theory of action is the only way to sustain an active reform agenda from one board-superintendent team to the next. It may take only 2 or 3 years for a reform board-superintendent team to show significant increases in elementary school student achievement, but it takes a decade or more for even the strongest reform team to establish firmly an aligned set of high-performance systems and create a district culture of performance.

Few board-superintendent teams serve for that long. Superintendents, on average, serve less than 6 years. Few serve 10 or more. And seldom does a board election pass without at least one new board member. A decade after the launch of a bold, comprehensive reform program, a district is likely to find itself with a new superintendent and an almost entirely new board of education.

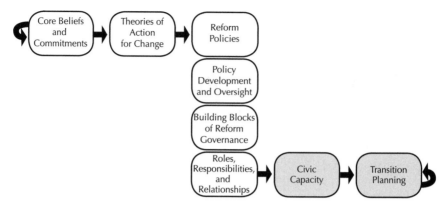

Figure 9.1. Civic capacity and transition planning as elements of Reform Governance Framework.

What can board members do to increase the likelihood that their successors will embrace and advance their reform program? They can do two things: first, make certain strong reform candidates committed to continuing on the same path seek to replace them and second, make voters prefer these candidates to others. The only way to carry out this plan is to build support for the board's reform program among business and civic elites, educate voters, develop a pool of potential reform candidates, and plan for change.

BUILDING CIVIC CAPACITY

Civic capacity is defined as the ability of a community to support the fundamental and enduring redesign of its school district for the purpose of eliminating the achievement gap. Every center of influence and every voter counts, but in most cities there are seven overlapping centers of influence that are critical: business leaders; elected officials (especially the mayor); parent activists; the media; and, in some cities, religious leaders, foundation leaders, and the local education fund. Most of these centers of influence have a major stake in the success of the school district, but without the leadership of the board of education, it is almost impossible for them to work in concert and sustain a commitment to action over long periods.

Business

In recent decades, especially since standards-based reform has brought to the attention of business leaders how poorly schools are performing, such leaders in more and more cities have mobilized to support school reform. In fact, in every city where significant improvement has occurred, business leaders have made a significant contribution, sometimes informally, frequently through formal organizations. However, business involvement in many cities has had minimal impact, because business leaders don't know how to leverage their power and because business has a short attention span.

Business leaders sometimes focus on the wrong thing—teaching and learning. They have little credibility or expertise in this area and few opportunities to leverage districtwide change. Except for individual school-business partnerships that bring businesspeople into schools for tutoring or other purposes or to fund instructional programs, there is little they can do to directly improve student achievement.

What business has in abundance and something most districts need is expertise to help district people create world-class business operations. Here, business leaders have credibility, expertise, and access. Superintendents and district operations people usually welcome business assistance. For them, it is free consulting.

However, the most powerful lever for change in the hands of business leaders is the political one. Although sometimes they would like to, business leaders cannot assume the powers of governance. They simply cannot work around the board of education. They can, however, significantly influence who is elected. Business influence and money has been the key to the election of numerous reform-minded school board members in many major cities. In a few cities, major district reform initiatives began with business action to recruit and elect a reform majority to the board of education.

The problem with business leadership is attention span. A crisis—a botched superintendent search, major business scandal, loss of state accreditation, or one more year of unacceptable student achievement on the state accountability system—brings forth business intervention. For a season, business leaders have a powerful influence on board elections, superintendent selection, and major district decisions. But time passes, stability is restored, key business leaders move on, and attention drifts. After all, business leaders have companies to manage. A couple of school board elections come and go with no business intervention, perhaps a superintendent retires, and years later new business leaders suddenly discover they have an educational crisis in their city.

Recognizing the long-term value of business involvement and the tendency of business leaders to focus attention on other priorities when school districts are not in crisis, Duval's Wilkinson recommends that boards formally promote involvement whether it appears to be needed or not. "Boards," she says, "need to approve policies and put into place processes that will ensure the continued involvement of business leaders. Advisory committees, periodic reports, regularly scheduled luncheons, or other formal processes are needed" (personal communication, January 4, 2005).

Elected Officials

Mayors matter, usually a lot. And often, city council members or state legislators have significant influence. In some cities, mayors or city councils appoint school board members. In these cities, they are more than centers of influence; in effect, they share governance power. This is also true where city councils or other elected bodies have the power to approve budgets. But even where there is no legal link between the mayor or other elected officials and the school board, these elected officials have power bases and enormous influence. And frequently they work hand in glove with business leaders.

Like business leaders, they also have a lot of other things on their mind. Their attention span might not be short, for they are always there and always interested; the problem is that they are also elected and have challenges to confront and constituents to keep happy. Like business leaders, they respond to crises and, in alliance with business leaders, their influence can be decisive, but unless school board members keep reaching out, educating, and involving them, the attention of elected officials also drifts.

Parent Activists

Parent activists—who frequently are stay-at-home professional women who have chosen to devote their time to homemaking and child rearing, but who increasingly are also fathers and working parents—focus sharply and unrelentingly on the district as long as they have children in school. They are great allies of board leaders because they have knowledge of the schools, a strong incentive for improvement, and adequate time. Few board members neglect them, for they provide most of the ground troops for school board elections. Their weakness is that although they know some schools well and are interested in a hundred small things, few understand major systems issues.

For most school boards, business leaders, elected officials, and parent activists are the three most powerful centers of influence in the city. When aligned, they can make almost anything happen. But there are other power centers that cannot be neglected.

Media

All urban districts have to contend with mass-circulation newspapers and major television networks. As noted in Chapter 5, the media are always a challenge. Despite their rhetoric about being guardians of democracy—seekers for truth on behalf of the people—mass-media companies are for-profit businesses that measure success with advertising revenues driven by circulation and viewer ratings. Like political conservatives, they seem to enjoy attacking urban districts for waste and corruption—waste and fraud in the public schools, like violent crime, attract viewers.

Even the most objective and sympathetic reporters and editors have a job to do, and it is reporting the news, not helping the school district build civic capacity. Board members must accept that in most cities, newspapers and television stations are not power centers to be educated and won over; they are power centers to be managed.

Religious Leaders, Foundation Executives, and Local Education Funds

Many cities have influential religious leaders—most frequently pastors of large African American churches—involved foundation executives, and an active local education fund. Where these centers of influence exist, they deserve great attention. The support or lack thereof of powerful pastors can make or break a school board candidate in electoral districts with large African American populations. Foundation executives in some cities—Pittsburgh, for example—have sparked major reform initiatives. And in some cities, the local education fund (LEF) is a major player.

LEFs have sprung up in many major cities to stimulate school reform that benefits low-income and minority students. LEFs are not-for-profit organizations supported by a combination of foundation dollars and local contributions that are used to increase the effectiveness and visibility of school and district improvement efforts. They provide direct service to students and professional development opportunities to teachers and principals and leverage local leadership and resources to sustain effective policy development and practice over time. In some cities, Boston and Portland, for example, by virtue of brilliant leadership and strong philanthropic support, they have become powerful forces for district improvement. More than 60 LEFs are members of the umbrella national organization the Public Education Network (Public Education Network, 2004).

Board Leadership for Civic Capacity

These powerful centers of influence and others have a critical role to play in the sustained improvement of a city's public schools. Without them, a board-superintendent team cannot long maintain a reform agenda. But none of these centers of influence can replace the board of education.

All other centers of influence, except for the LEF and parent activists, have other priorities to distract them. None of the others, except for elected officials, has the same grasp of politics. And none can reach around the board of education to make policy and oversee management.

However much other groups from time to time might claim to represent the interests of children or the public, where boards are elected, only the board has the democratic authority to speak for the people. And only the board is at the nexus where all the vectors of influence meet. The board of education has the responsibility, the sharp focus on education and only education, and the power. For all these reasons, the board of education, and only the board of education, can pull together a city's major centers of influence into a loose coalition with a common vision and maintain constancy of purpose over time. And also, for all these same reasons, over the long haul, elected boards have an advantage over appointed boards.

What needs to be done? First, the public must believe that the district is honestly and openly acknowledging its problems and making concerted efforts to improve. Too many urban districts have minimized problems, made excuses, and put the blame for failures on individuals rather than acknowledged that problems are serious and systems ineffective.

It is difficult to balance advocacy with acknowledgment of failures, especially when some attacks are unfair, politically motivated district bashing. Nevertheless, striking this balance is essential. Spirited responses to disinformation are sometimes required. These are all the more believable when they occur within a pattern of honest, open communication about district failures, along with steps the district is taking to respond to failures and improve systems.

Second, the public must also understand the board's core beliefs and commitments, theory of action, and policy framework. Building on a foundation of trust created by honest and open communication about what *is*, the board must build support for what *should be*.

It is not realistic to expect more than a few informed parents and voters to understand the theory and practice of urban school reform or to be able to repeat phrases from the board's vision statement. However, most active parents and regular voters should know that the district is committed to eliminating the achievement gap and is involved in a major reform initiative that is designed to accomplish this. And they should be able to identify the essence of the board's theory of action—a more tightly managed instructional system, or more accountability for results, or the creation of more charter schools, or other goals.

Selected business leaders, elected officials, parent leaders, members of the newspaper's editorial board, and others should know more. They should be able to give at least an elevator speech—about all the time most listeners will give—outlining the district's goals, strategy, and most recent policy initiatives. Building this level of understanding and commitment is a time-consuming and never-ending task, but it must be done. And no one can do it better than the board of education.

Indeed, the superintendent is a powerful member of the governance team and the spokesperson for the district. Urban superintendents are major public persons. Board members usually are not. Superintendents have immediate access to the media and every major center of influence in the city. Board members seldom do. Superintendents are like queens on a chessboard. They have more power and influence than any other person on or off the board of education, and they are point persons for building civic capacity.

Board members, however, have deep community roots and, collectively, especially if they are elected, know virtually every influential person in the city and thousands of people who are only influential in neighborhoods. They can be in many different places at the same time, and everywhere they can talk with credibility about what exists and what needs to be done. Collectively, they are the public's best teacher. Furthermore, they are the representatives of the people, and it is their responsibility to educate the public.

Together a board-superintendent team can design and implement a powerful strategy to build civic capacity. The superintendent's job, with full board support, is to create a district infrastructure that includes highly effective people and systems to manage media relations, community partnerships, and parent involvement and to personally be an evangelist for the board's vision for change.

Board members, coordinating their work with the superintendent and one another, must continually reach out to groups and individuals to build personal relationships and educate, educate, educate. Specifically, board members need to map centers and people of influence in the city, make assignments, and maintain up-to-date records of conversations and commitments. Let Republican board members take responsibility for courting Republican activists. Let Democratic board members do the same with Democrats. Let board members with contacts in the business community, ethnic communities, or any other communities take responsibility for nurturing relationships and building support for reform.

Board members should request that the board services office create a speakers' bureau so board members can systematically reach out to chamber of commerce organizations, service and civic clubs, professional and trade associations, and church or educational groups. If some group is looking for speakers, let them know that board members are effective public speakers and have a great story to tell. So by e-mail and print newsletters, speeches, breakfasts and lunches, phone calls and conversations in the corridors of power, or wherever people will listen, board members need to reach out, win friends, and influence people.

To do this effectively, board members must continually deepen their knowledge of urban school reform and the reform program in their district, continuously develop their skills as communicators, and coordinate their talking points with one another and the superintendent in a coordinated outreach strategy. And they must work as if there is an election just ahead, for there always is.

With hard work and good fortune, the result of this outreach is that influential business leaders, elected officials, parent groups, and others with influence understand and embrace the board's core beliefs and commitments and theory of action, and a majority of the voters believe that the district is moving in the right direction. With this understanding and support, board-superintendent teams can lead fundamental district redesign, overcome powerful resistance to change, and even build support for more resources.

TRANSITION PLANNING

One of life's great truths is that all of us are transitional. Superintendents come and go; so do board members and civic and community leaders. Periods of stability mask transitions going on under the surface, just as periods of instability mask how little change is taking place in classrooms and schools. Change is constant, but it does alter course and speed, especially when leadership changes.

School boards practicing reform governance want dramatic change and are frustrated by how difficult it is to alter the direction of urban districts. Like great ocean liners, urban districts alter their direction slowly. Precisely because school districts are so hard to turn, school boards in the midst of transition, however frustrated they might be by the pace of change, cannot take the risk that new leaders will change course. This is exactly what all too often happens.

Paul Hill and colleagues (1998) and Rick Hess (1999) have documented the impact of departing superintendents on promising reform initiatives and the policy churn that characterizes urban districts as new superintendents and board members abandon the reform policies of their predecessors in order to put their stamp on new and unaligned reform policies. One can point to periods of reform energy and rising student achievement under strong superintendent-board teams in a dozen major urban districts. How many districts can one name in which three, even two, strong superintendents and gradually changing board teams have acted effectively on the same theory of action and implemented aligned reform policies within the same policy framework?

Reform board-superintendent teams can make significant improvements in urban districts in 3 or 4 years and obtain improvements in elementary reading or math test scores in even 2. But deep systemic change and the creation of a performance culture require at least 10 years. Even then, the journey has just begun. Because reform takes time, stability is preferred. Rapid board and superintendent turnover is the enemy of sustainable change. Assuming a district has a board-superintendent team moving together down a reform path, the fewer leadership changes the better.

Stability starts with the board of education. Community leaders should encourage effective board members to commit themselves to long-term service on the board of education. This is a sacrifice, for board service eats into family time and can slow professional advancement. But sacrifice is required for all great endeavors.

Board members become more effective as they gain experience. At least second terms, and third terms where possible, are needed. Stable boards reduce superintendent turnover, and stable board-superintendent teams increase the likelihood of deep, sustainable reform.

Julian Treviño, who has made a personal commitment to stability in San Antonio, states his commitment this way:

> Seeing firsthand the value of longevity for board and superintendent, I recently committed myself to a third term, and I have made it a priority to encourage stability on the San Antonio board. We have made a good start, but we have so much more to do. (Personal communication, December 24, 2004)

Stability is critical, but transition planning is still necessary. Even stable boards have turnover. Even long-serving superintendents eventually move on. Even business and civic leaders, the most stable of these three centers of power, change jobs or retire. No one generation of reformers can transform an urban district. It is the work of a succession of gradually changing leaders. Managing this succession requires succession planning.

The board-superintendent team has responsibility for succession planning for the superintendency and major management positions within the district. Board members, with the help of the superintendent and civic leaders, are responsible for the cultivation and recruitment of outstanding citizens for board elections. And business and civic leaders must accept responsibility for constantly renewing the city's leadership.

Civic capacity enables succession planning to become effective succession management. A board-superintendent team that has built civic capacity reaps its reward when school board elections are fought on the issue of which candidate will most effectively provide leadership for accelerating the reform trajectory and when the public supports the selection of a new superintendent committed to advancing what is now the city's theory of action.

Board of Education

Consider school board elections. Most urban districts with elected boards have board elections every 2 years, though patterns vary. Come election season, the first question that buzzes among district watchers is, Will incumbent board member John or Susan Smith seek reelection? If so, and if John or Susan has been an excellent or even fair trustee, reelection is likely.

This does not mean John or Susan will not have an opponent. All sorts of people, sometimes rather strange people, come out of nowhere to seek election to urban school boards. More often than not, however, reasonably effective incumbent board members do not draw well-known, widely respected, well-funded opponents.

Of course, it sometimes happens. Recent controversy, a major issue, or a power struggle involving special interests—for example, a financial debacle, the closing of a high school, or an unhappy teachers union—can force an incumbent trustee into a tight race with a credible opponent. Highly effective board members are from time to time taken out. When this happens, the issue is usually not the performance of the trustee; it is a controversial issue or the performance or direction of the district.

When an incumbent does not seek reelection, the election is also frequently about the direction of the district. Of course, candidate quality matters, but candidates run on issues. And though there are almost always specific issues in the air, the major issue in most urban board elections—like the overriding issue in most presidential elections—is whether voters believe that the district is moving in the right direction.

In urban America, few candidates challenging an incumbent trustee or seeking an open seat on the city's board of education run on a platform pledging to support the district's current direction. They run as critics. They blast low student achievement, high drop-out rates, incompetence, waste, and frequently the neglect of their community or neighborhood.

A district passes the acid test of public knowledge and support for its vision and achievement when strong credible candidates rise up to challenge negative board members or seek election to open seats, vying with one another over who will work most effectively with the board-superintendent team to keep the district on its chosen path. Boards with a clear theory of action, a record of achievement, and a reputation for collegial working relationships should have no trouble passing this test.

Superintendents

Boards with a clear reform agenda seek to replace departing superintendents with successors who understand and are deeply committed to the board's core beliefs and commitments and theory of action and who welcome the board's leadership for reform and active involvement in the development of reform policies. However, finding such a successor is difficult if the departing superintendent has not prepared the way by working with the board to plan for his or her departure.

This is hard for many superintendents to do. Like many corporate CEOs, they have a difficult time thinking about their departure, let alone planning for it. But everyone, sooner or later, moves on, and it is a big mistake for boards to allow their superintendent to dodge this issue.

What should board-superintendent teams do? First, boards with effective reform leaders in the superintendent's chair should do everything in their power to keep them there. Provide fair compensation (and superintendents who can improve the performance of urban districts deserve plenty). Provide high-quality and sufficient quantity of staff so that the superintendent can work a reasonable work week and have time to contribute to the national debate on improving urban schools and enjoy personal growth. Show appreciation. And don't fret over minor flaws. No one is perfect.

Second, insist that the superintendent build a leadership team that includes potential successors. Replacements from within are preferred. They know the district, and their competence and commitment to the vision for change can be assessed. Great companies in the private sector normally replace CEOs from within, except when a change of direction is desired. A board moving down a reform path does not want a change of direction.

Identifying an heir apparent is a mistake. It is not good for the superintendent, the district, or the designated heir. Although planning for the future is important, the focus of work for everyone in the district must be the present. Districts need several potential superintendent candidates on the superintendent's leadership team, not just one.

Every year, when the board evaluates the superintendent and sets goals for the coming year, the board should require the superintendent to assess the leadership potential of his or her direct reports, or selected other senior administrators in the district, and outline plans for the leadership development of these people. In addition, the superintendent should provide board members with ongoing opportunities to observe the performance of these people.

What, some will cry, is it not micromanagement for board members to be involved in personnel management? Should not superintendents be unrestrained in their freedom to appoint, assign, and evaluate employees? After all, the board holds the superintendent, and the superintendent alone, responsible for the performance of the district. How can the board involve itself in appointments and assessments of the superintendent's leadership team?

This is tricky work, to be sure. It is not something boards should do in the first years of a new superintendent. At that point they have their hands full evaluating the superintendent, and trust levels may not be high enough to support this level of candor and confidentiality. In time, however, with a focus only on potential for districtwide leadership, not on current performance, superintendents and boards must act strategically and talk candidly about the future, for the future will eventually come.

Succession planning should not cause stress, for boards and superintendents have the same need for a smooth transition. Boards, because they have continuing responsibility for the district, and superintendents, because they have a legacy to protect, have a common goal: a successor superintendent who will, in his or her own unique way, continue on the same reform path.

Management

Transition planning is for more than superintendents. It is for all those in senior positions, including principals. Just as boards should work with superintendents on superintendent succession planning, boards should require superintendents to build succession planning into their districts' processes and culture. Organizations managing change benefit when vacancies are filled by successors who understand and are committed to the change process.

Business and Civic Leaders

Just as board members should plan for their own succession, so should business and civic leaders. Although such figures as business leaders, elected officials, foundation and other not-for-profit executives, and pastors may remain at the center of influence for decades or more, as mentioned above, they have many priorities competing for their attention. Expecting all of them to make school district improvement their priority year after year is unrealistic.

Somehow, cities must find a way to keep at least a core of civic leaders unrelentingly focused on school reform. For every civic leader who retires, moves, or shifts his or her priority to something else, another must be recruited to the cause. The individuals best suited for this work are those who currently lead. Maintaining a fresh supply of civic leaders willing to put time and energy into urban school reform should not, however, be left entirely to those who currently lead. A powerful ally in this work—in fact, the one person who should make it one of his or her top responsibilities—is the mayor.

All cities have mayors. All mayors have an enormous stake in the performance of the public schools. And all mayors are elected and from time to time need the support of those with influence.

Board members have influence, and they can almost always obtain the ear of the mayor or those who want to be mayor. Let them, in the most politically acceptable and effective way, work with and through their mayors, or directly if they have personal influence, to constantly refresh the school reform leadership of their cities' business and civic elites. Only those cities whose business and civic elites have a relentless and never ending focus on high performance can hope to create and sustain high-performing school districts.

CHAPTER 10

Board Leadership

REFORM GOVERNANCE IS A NEW WAY of looking at the work of urban school boards. Its premise is that fundamental redesign of urban districts is required to educate all children to grade level and to their potential and to eliminate the achievement gap and that fundamental redesign requires the leadership of the board of education.

The administrative progressives of the early decades of the 20th century created an efficient and robust design for urban school districts to meet the needs of America in 1920. This system, which in their minds was the one best system, Americanized the nation's new immigrants and educated most children through eighth grade, preparing them for unskilled work or on-the-job training for more highly skilled jobs. Its high schools funneled a sufficient number of youths (although most of them were White males from middle-class families) into college, business leadership, and the professions.

The system was not moral, for it discriminated against poor children, children of color, and girls, but it accomplished its purpose. Like the factory system on which it was based, it efficiently moved cohorts of children through the grades, cutting, shaping, polishing, and spitting out what American elites believed their democracy and the labor market needed.

We know today that we need something quite different. American democracy is now more fully realized. We recognize that the promise of democracy is the promise that all children—boys or girls, rich or poor, White or some other color, healthy or disabled—deserve a quality education and the opportunity to reach as high as their talents can take them. The workplace has also changed. Fewer and fewer workers are needed in agriculture and manufacturing. Work for strong backs has given way to work for strong minds. The information technology revolution and globalization have changed the world and the world of work.

We have changed the way we communicate, travel, provide health care, and produce most of the goods and services we consume. It is past time to change the way we educate children in America's great cities. What we need are new designs for America's urban school districts.

In the theories of action that are driving new district designs we can already see the shape of the future. Managed instruction, with its focus on curriculum, professional development, formative assessments, student information systems, and timely interventions, brings the quality-management principles of process analysis and improvement to education. Performance/empowerment, built on another quality-management principle—the core idea that workers will innovate and strive for high performance if they are empowered and held accountable for results—aligns the interests of teachers and principals with the needs of children. Managed empowerment/performance blends these two theories of action by managing instruction with flexibility and giving schools control of almost everything else, balancing performance-based accountability for school management with various levels of performance-based and compliance-based accountability for instruction. Charter districts, a powerful but untried idea, rely on consumer choice and provider competition in a regulated educational market to create good schools for all children.

These theories of action are built on assumptions, ideas, principles, and emerging experience. They will no doubt be refined and blended in various ways in the coming 2 decades to create new district designs for the 21st century. Whatever these new designs may look like, there are already some things we can say about the urban districts of the future.

- They will be designed to educate all children to grade level and to potential and to eliminate the achievement gap.
- They will guarantee equity, defined as unequal resources for unequal needs.
- They will make extensive use of information technology for business management, instructional management, tracking students, and instruction.
- Although children may be in classes, they will be educated as individuals, not as members of a class. Information technology and instructional technology will make possible individualized instruction, variable rather than fixed schedules for learning, and variable units of learning.
- There will be content standards; a focused, aligned, and comprehensive curriculum; performance standards, formative assessments, and summative assessments of student performance. In short, districts will know exactly what they want children to learn and how well children are learning.
- Because teachers will remain the indispensable key to student learning, they will receive intense professional development focused sharply on content, curriculum, and pedagogy.
- In addition, because teachers will remain the indispensable key to student learning, they will enter the teaching profession in multiple ways; be deployed, evaluated, and compensated in variable ways; and have less job security but more professional choice, higher status, and higher pay.

- Although the instructional core of schools will be tightly managed by school districts, schools will have more control over budgets, personnel, schedules, procurement, and so on and will shape themselves around unique themes to differentiate themselves in the marketplace.
- Districts and schools will be increasingly subject to marketplace forces: They will compete for students, and parents will have significantly more choice.
- Performance will be measured in ever more sophisticated ways, and managers, teachers, and students will be held accountable for performance.
- Schools will be more deeply imbedded in the communities they serve and more tightly linked with other public and private institutions that serve youth.

Why am I so confident that urban districts will be redesigned around these principles? There are ample reasons to be pessimistic about the future, and failure is always an option. But I don't think America will fail. The stakes are too high. Americans have always risen to meet great challenges. I don't think they will fail to meet the challenge of educating all children.

To meet this challenge, I am convinced that high-performing urban districts are required. Not all agree. Let those who don't pursue other solutions. But look at urban America. Where are the children? In the public schools. Charter schools and voucher programs will not educate this generation of America's urban children. School districts will. This is why making them high-performing organizations is the nation's highest domestic priority.

Given the cogency of the theories of action being put forward by practitioners, theorists, and policy makers; the results achieved to date; and the experience of history that human institutions evolve from known to unknown, if urban districts improve, they are most likely to do so by elaborating on the redesign principles currently being used. And because institutions improve by borrowing from similar institutions in other economic sectors, it is likely that school districts will borrow organizational and performance principles from the business sector, employ technology more extensively and effectively, and subject themselves, willingly or unwillingly, to the forces of the marketplace.

Who will redesign school districts for the 21st century? The same people who have pioneered performance/empowerment, managed instruction, managed performance/empowerment, and charter districts: practitioners and policy makers. Redesign ideas will come from many sources. School people, however, assisted by business and community volunteers, will be the people who actually do the difficult, complex, detailed work of redesign.

What about boards? They will contribute some redesign ideas, and in their policy-development work get involved in some redesign work. But their major contribution will be as reform leaders. What specifically will they do, must they do? Urban district board members must create broad public support for all children learning at high levels, embrace a cogent theory of action for how to make this happen, and put into place a policy framework of aligned reform policies. To do this they must build productive relationships and practices and understand their proper role in management oversight, constituent service, and policy development and oversight. In short, they must practice reform governance.

Without reform governance, urban district redesign will not happen. The changes required are so broad and deep that sustained democratic support over the tenures of several superintendents is required. Only school boards, because of their deep roots in the communities they serve, the democratic power they exercise on behalf of the people, and their continuity over decades can lead and sustain changes this deep and this enduring.

Reform governance is not a blueprint showing how to make this happen. No blueprint is possible. Context is everything. Every district is unique. What, then, is reform governance? It is a theory of governance, a guide to action, a framework for understanding the work of a reform board. It is comprehensive, but not complete—comprehensive because it comprehends the entirety of the work of a reform board and shows the relationships among all the elements, incomplete because it does not catalog the scores of additional activities within the reform governance elements that fill the time of urban school board members.

This book is an explication of reform governance, a theory placed for understanding in a conceptual framework. The Reform Governance Framework presents reform governance theory as a flowchart standing above the governance/management line. The boxes in the flowchart represent the board's work. The governance/management line and the up and down arrows represent the relationship between the board and superintendent.

Because beliefs and commitments are the foundation for action, reform governance and this book start logically with core beliefs and commitments. Reform governance affirms that a commitment to all children performing at grade level and to potential and the elimination of the achievement gap is the starting point for board leadership for district redesign.

Core beliefs and commitments feed directly into the theories of action for change, because change leadership is not possible unless leaders not only know where they want to go but also have an overarching idea of how they will get there. Just as value propositions lead to business models, so in school districts a theory of action sets forth the principles for district redesign.

The four comprehensive theories of action for transforming urban districts described in this book are not put forward as the only options available to boards. They are the ones currently showing the most promise in urban districts. Of the four, managed performance/empowerment appears to be the most powerful option within political reach, but in the coming decade, mixed-portfolio districts, which combine managed performance/empowerment with charter districts, may emerge as the preferred model. The reform governance point is not that one of these change theories for district redesign must be accepted; it is simply that boards must have a change theory if they are to lead change.

A theory of action makes possible a coherent change process, but it will not transform an urban district. Policies are the instruments of change and, along with superintendent selection and the bully pulpit, are the most powerful levers available to a reform board.

Reform policies spring from a board's theory of action, but before a board can provide effective reform policy leadership, it must work together as an effective team with its superintendent. This entails a clear understanding of roles and responsibilities, positive working relationships, and effective processes for board work, especially effective policy-development work.

Board members have numerous relationship spheres. The most important relationships are, of course, those among board members and the key relationship with the superintendent. Reform governance makes recommendations for effective relationships in all these spheres, especially on how to manage best the two most problematic issues in board-superintendent relations: constituent service and management oversight.

There are many processes through which boards do their work. The major ones are board meetings, board workshops, board committees, and the supporting work of the board services department. No board can provide effective reform leadership if these processes are dysfunctional. Again, based on best practices, reform governance makes recommendations.

Policy development, approval, and oversight are the key processes through which boards transform districts. It is important for boards to make a distinction between routine operating policies and reform policies, to understand the principles and methods of policy development, and to recognize that the board's work is not done when policies are approved. Policies must be monitored for implementation and evaluated for results.

Policy content is where all the elements of reform governance come together. All the work of reform governance points to this objective: the right combination of aligned reform policies properly implemented. Chapter 8, in which I briefly outline the policy framework for the comprehensive theories of action presented in Chapter 4, provides board members with examples of the policies that are currently helping to transform the highest-performing urban districts in America. But again, as with theories of action, the reform governance point is not that reform boards must select reform policies from among those presented; it is that reform boards must approve reform policies. That is their primary job.

Building civic capacity and transition planning are the final two elements in the reform governance theory. They are required because school districts are an integral part of their communities, owned by and answerable to the citizens. Governance as oversight needs a link with the public; governance for change requires broad public understanding and support. Boards must work without ceasing to educate civic elites on their core beliefs and commitments and theory of action. And because transforming an urban district takes a decade or more and because superintendents, board members, and even civic leaders are transitional leaders, boards must take responsibility for transition planning.

The elements of reform governance are represented in boxes in the Reform Governance Framework, but of course, as stated before, in the real life of board members, work cannot be separated into boxes. Everything is happening at the same time. Chaos often prevails. It is frequently difficult to obtain consensus on anything important. No theory of action consistently guides the development of reform policies. Conventions on major board processes are not agreed upon or are in constant flux. And no one seems to know for certain, or else everyone has a different idea, about the powers and responsibilities of the board.

Notwithstanding messy reality and the limitations of a static, two-dimensional model to describe it, the Reform Governance Framework is put forward with the hope that board members will use it as a tool to help them understand their work and to guide their actions as reform leaders.

Several vital questions remain. Who can do such work? Can urban America find the board members it needs to lead in the transformation of urban districts? Will men and women with the vision, talent, courage, integrity, and time step forward to seek election to urban boards? Will the voters prefer these candidates to others? Where boards are appointed, will mayors or the individuals who make appointments appoint such candidates and give them the democratic mandate and political cover to lead reform?

If so, reform governance offers a pathway to high achievement for all children. Applied and modified in various ways to meet the unique needs of time and place, the principles of reform governance, brought alive by the actions of board leaders for reform, will enable cities to create high-performing school districts and good schools for all their children.

Public schools are democratic institutions. Like all democratic institutions, they are owned by the people. The people, through their tax dollars, pay the bills, and those who vote directly or indirectly elect those who govern. Americans have the schools they have chosen for themselves. If they want good schools for all children, if they want high-performing school districts, if they want high achievement for all children, they have it in their power to make it so. The place to start is the voting booth, where reform leaders can be elected to boards of education. This is a job for the people, and especially for civic elites. Reform governance is the work of school boards. Improving America's urban schools is everyone's responsibility.

Notes

CHAPTER 4

1. A word on nomenclature is appropriate. *Performance/empowerment*, my term, is a shortened form of *performance-based empowerment*, a more accurate, if cumbersome, phrase. Educators sometimes use the words *accountability* and *decentralization*, but *accountability* does not capture the idea that it is performance, not only being accountable, that justifies empowerment. And *empowerment*, unlike *decentralization*, suggests only that schools are given the power necessary to do the job, not the diminution of Central Office power. *Managed Instruction* is not yet a universally recognized term, but it is rapidly gaining currency.

2. The work product to date, published in the *Portfolio for District Redesign* (School Communities That Work, 2002), includes eight essays, starting with an overview essay: "School Communities that Work for Results and Equity." The other seven are "Generally Accepted Principles of Teaching and Learning"; "Central Office Review for Results and Equity"; "Find, Deploy, Support, and Keep the Best Teachers and School Leaders"; "Developing Effective Partnerships to Support Local Education"; "First Steps to a Level Playing Field: An Introduction to Student-Based Budgeting"; "Assessing Inequities in School Funding Within Districts: A Tool to Prepare for Student-Based Budgeting"; and "Moving Toward Equity in School Funding Within Districts."

CHAPTER 7

1. I am indebted to John Carver's excellent books on policy governance for these principles. I am not following him exactly, but I am dependent on his pioneering work in this area. See Carver, 1997, 2001, 2002 and Carver and Carver, 1997.

CHAPTER 8

1. For an examination of these issues, principles for implementation, and a survey of school district accountability systems, including extended essays on three

systems (Boston, Cincinnati, and Houston), see McAdams et al., 2002. This section on district accountability systems borrows freely from that report.

2. Karen Hawley Miles and Marguerite Roza have produced the best scholarship on weighted student funding. See, for instance, Roza & Hawley Miles, 2002a, 2002b, 2002c. Former superintendents Mike Strembitsky (Edmonton), Joseph Olchefske (Seattle), Rod Paige (Houston), and Steven Adamowski (Cincinnati) are experts.

References

Allen, J., Cotter, M. E., & Marcucio, A. V. (2003). *Charter schools today: Changing the face of American education: Statistics, stories and impacts.* Washington, DC: The Center for Education Reform.

Anderson, G. (2000). *Malcolm Baldrige: A quality and effective framework: A Texas school district's perspective* (Slide presentation). Brazosport, TX: Brazosport Independent School District. Available: http://www.dcccd.edu/qfq/pp/sld001.htm

Balfanz, R., & Letgers, N. (2004). *Which high schools produce the nation's dropouts? Where are they located? Who attends them?* Baltimore, MD: Johns Hopkins University, Center for Social Organization of Schools.

Boston Public Schools. (2004). *Six essentials for whole school improvement.* Available: http://www.boston.k12.ma.us/teach/offices.pdf

Braswell, J., Daane, M., & Grigg, W. (2003). *The nation's report card: Mathematics highlights 2003.* Washington, DC: National Assessment of Educational Progress, U.S. Department of Education, Institute of Education Sciences, National Center for Education Statistics. Available: http://nces.ed.gov/pubsearch/pubsinfo.asp?pubid=2004451

Bulkley, K., & Fisler, J. (2002). *A review of the research on charter schools.* Philadelphia: University of Pennsylvania, Consortium for Policy Research in Education.

Campbell, C. (2002). *San Diego City Schools: Breaking eggs: Omelet or scrambled?* (Unpublished case study prepared for the Broad Institute for School Boards). Houston, TX: Center for Reform of School Systems.

Campbell, J. R., Hombo, C. R., & Mazzeo, J. (2000). *NAEP 1999: Trends in academic progress: Three decades of student performance.* Washington, DC: U.S. Department of Education, National Center for Education Statistics.

Carver, J. (1997). *Boards that make a difference: A new design for leadership in non-profit and public organizations* (2nd ed.). San Francisco: Jossey-Bass.

Carver, J. (2001). *John Carver on board leadership: Selected writings from the creator of the world's most provocative and systematic governance model.* San Francisco: Jossey-Bass.

Carver, J. (2002). *Corporate boards that create value: Governing company performance from the boardroom.* San Francisco: Jossey-Bass.

Carver, J., & Carver, M. M. (1997). *Reinventing your board: A step-by-step guide to implementing policy governance.* San Francisco: Jossey-Bass.

Casserly, M. (2004). *Beating the odds IV*. Washington, DC: Council of the Great City Schools.

Cincinnati Public Schools. (1996). *Students first* (Strategic plan adopted December 9, 1996). Cincinnati, OH: Author.

Coleman, J. S. (1986). Social theory, social research, and a theory of action. *American Journal of Sociology, 91*(6), 1309–1335.

Coleman, J. S., et al. (1966). *Equality of educational opportunity*. Washington, DC: U.S. Government Printing Office.

Council of the Great City Schools. (2002). *Council of the Great City Schools and the nation, 2001–2002*. Available: http://www.cgcs.org/pdfs/Statistical_Information.pdf

Council of the Great City Schools. (2004). *Restoring excellence to the D.C. Public Schools*. Available: http://www.cgcs.org/pdfs/DCPSReportFinal.pdf

Cuban, L. (1993). *How teachers taught* (2nd ed.). New York: Teachers College Press.

Cuban, L., & Tyack, D. (1995). *Tinkering toward utopia: A century of public school reform*. Cambridge, MA: Harvard University Press.

Darling-Hammond, L., Hightower, A. M., Husbands, J. L., LaFors, J. R., Young, V. M., & Christopher, C. (2003). *Building instructional quality: "Inside-out" and "outside-in" perspectives on San Diego's school reform*. Seattle: University of Washington, Center for the Study of Teaching and Policy.

Donahue, P., Daane, M., & Grigg, W. (2003). *The nation's report card: Reading highlights 2003*. Washington, DC: National Assessment of Educational Progress, U.S. Department of Education, Institute of Education Sciences, National Center for Education Statistics. Available: http://nces.ed.gov/nationsreportcard/pdf/main2003/2004452.pdf

Drucker, P. (1974). *Management: Tasks, responsibilities, practice*. New York: Harper & Row.

Education Commission of the States. (1999). *Governing America's schools: Changing the rules*. Denver, CO: Education Commission of the States, National Commission on Governing America's Schools.

The Education Trust. (2002). *Dispelling the myth . . . over time*. Washington, DC: Author.

Elmore, R. (2000). *Building a new structure for school leadership*. New York: The Albert Shanker Institute.

Elmore, R., & Burney, D. (1997a). *Investing in teacher learning: Staff development and instructional improvement in Community School District #2, New York City*. New York: Columbia University, Teachers' College, National Commission on Teaching and America's Future.

Elmore, R., & Burney, D. (1997b). *School variation and systemic instructional improvement in Community School District #2, New York City: High Performance Learning Communities project*. Pittsburgh, PA: Pittsburgh University, Learning Research and Development Center.

Foley, E. (2001). *Contradictions and control in systemic reform: The ascendancy of the central office under Children Achieving*. Philadelphia: Consortium for Policy Research in Education.

Foley, E. (2002). *School district of Philadelphia: The man with the plan* (Unpublished case study prepared for the Broad Institute for School Boards). Houston, TX: Center for Reform of School Systems.

Foster, J. D. (1999). *Redesigning public education: The Kentucky experience.* Lexington, KY: Diversified Services.

Gemberling, K. W., Smith, C. W., & Villani, J. S. (2000). *The key work of school boards guidebook.* Alexandria, VA: National School Boards Association.

Gill, B. P., Timpane, P. M., Ross, K. E., & Brewer, D. J. (2001). *Rhetoric versus reality: What we know and what we need to know about vouchers and charter schools.* Santa Monica, CA: RAND.

Glass, T. E., Bjork, L., & Brunner, C. C. (2000). *The study of the American superintendency, 2000. A look at the superintendent of education in the new millennium.* Arlington, VA: American Association of School Administrators.

Goldhaber, D. D. (1999). School choice: An examination of the empirical evidence on achievement, parental decision making, and equity. *Educational Researcher, 28*(9), 16–25.

Goldstein, L. (2004). Long-awaited spec. ed. testing rules issued. *Education Week, 23*(16), 27–29.

Hadderman, M. (2002). *Public voucher plans.* Available: http://eric.uoregon.edu/trends_issues/choice/intersectional

Handcock, M., & Morris, M. (1999). *Relative distribution methods in the social sciences.* New York: Springer.

Hassel, B. (1999). *Charter schools: Policy success story begins to emerge.* Washington, DC: Progressive Policy Institute. Available: http://www.ppionline.org/ppi_ci.cfm?knlgAreaID=110&subsecID=134&contentID=676

Hawley Miles, K. (2002a). Cincinnati Public Schools accountability system: Strategic coherence and serious consequences. In D. McAdams, et al., *Urban school district accountability systems* (p. 33). Houston, TX: Center for Reform of School Systems.

Hawley Miles, K. (2002b). *Cincinnati Public Schools: Cutting the pie: Defining equity* (Unpublished case study prepared for the Broad Institute for School Boards). Houston, TX: Center for Reform of School Systems.

Hawley Miles, K. (2002c). A theory of action, a work in progress: Boston Public Schools' accountability system. In D. McAdams, et al., *Urban school district accountability systems* (p. 36). Houston, TX: Center for Reform of School Systems.

Haycock, K., Jerald, C., & Huang, S. (2001, Spring). Closing the gap: Done in a decade. *Thinking K–16* (p. 4). Available: http://www2.edtrust.org/NR/rdonlyres/85EB1387-A6B7-4AF4-BEB7-DF389772ECD2/0/k16_spring01.pdf

Hedges, L. V., & Nowell, A. (1998). Black-white test score convergence since 1965. In C. Jencks & M. Phillips (Eds.), *The black-white achievement gap* (pp. 149–181). Washington, DC: The Brookings Institution Press.

Henderson, C. (2000). *Vertical teaming yields vertical achievement in southeastern Texas school district* (Case study). Houston, TX: American Productivity & Quality Center.

Hess, F. M. (1999). *Spinning wheels: The politics of urban school reform.* Washington, DC: The Brookings Institution Press.

Hess, F. M. (Ed.). (2005). *Urban school reform: Lessons from San Diego.* Cambridge, MA: Harvard Education Press.

Hightower, A. (2002). *San Diego's big boom: District bureaucracy supports culture of learning.* Seattle: University of Washington, Center for the Study of Teaching and Policy.

Hill, P. T. (2001). *Charter school districts.* Washington, DC: Progressive Policy Institute. Available: http://www.ppionline.org/ppi_ci.cfm?contentid=3365&knlgAreaID=110&subsecid=134

Hill, P. T., Campbell, C., & Harvey, J. (2000). *It takes a city: Getting serious about urban school reform.* Washington, DC: The Brookings Institution Press.

Hill, P. T., Celio, M. B., & Harvey, J. (1998). *Fixing urban schools.* Washington, DC: The Brookings Institution Press.

Hornbeck, D. W. (1994). *Children achieving.* Philadelphia: School District of Philadelphia.

Houston Independent School District. (2001). *A declaration of beliefs and vision.* Available: http://www.houstonisd.org/HISD/portal/article/front/0,2731, 20856_2404_10202,00.html

Jencks, C., & Phillips, M. (Eds.). (1998). *The black-white test score gap.* Washington, DC: The Brookings Institution Press.

Jenkins, L. (2004). *Raising the bar: High standards and high stakes in Gwinnett County Public Schools* (Unpublished case study). Houston, TX: Center for Reform of School Systems.

Kentucky Education Reform Act, Kentucky State Legislature, House Bill 940 (1990).

Kentucky Institute for Education Research. (1996). *A review of research on the Kentucky Education Reform Act 1995 (KERA).* Frankfort: Kentucky University–Louisville University, Joint Center for the Study of Educational Policy.

Leal, D. (2000, October 23–24). *Shared decision making councils in Houston's public schools.* Paper presented at the "Making the Grade" conference, Houston, TX.

Leschly, S. (2002). *Transformation of Seattle Public Schools: 1995–2002* (Case study). Cambridge, MA: Harvard Business School. Available: http://harvardbusinessonline.hbsp.harvard.edu/b02/en/includes/search/search_results.jhtml?_requestid=28235

Loveless, T. (2003). *Brown Center report on American education.* Washington, DC: The Brookings Institution Press.

McAdams, D., Wisdom, M., Glover, S., & McClellan, A. (2002). *Urban school district accountability systems.* Houston, TX: Center for Reform of School Systems. Available: http://www.ecs.org/html/educationissues/accountability/mcadams_report.pdf

McAdams, D. R. (2002). Houston ISD: An improving accountability system to support whole systems change. In D. McAdams et al. (Ed.), *Urban school district accountability systems* (pp. 39–47). Houston, TX: Center for Reform of School Systems.

McAdams, D. R., & Breier, B. B. (2003). *It takes a city: Building a high performance school district in Houston* (Unpublished case study prepared for the

Broad Institute for School Boards). Houston, TX: Center for Reform of School Systems.

Mehrotra, S. (2000). *Integrating economic and social policy: Good practices from high-achieving countries* (No. 80). Florence: UNICEF Innocenti Research Centre.

Mirel, J. (1999). Urban public schools in the 20th century: The view from Detroit. In D. Ravitch (Ed.), *Brookings papers on education policy: 1999*. Washington, DC: The Brookings Institution Press.

National Assessment of Educational Progress. (2003). *Percentage of students by reading achievement level, grades 4 and 8 public schools: By urban district, 2002 and 2003*. Washington, DC: U.S. Department of Education, Institute of Education Sciences, National Center for Education Statistics.

National Center for Educational Accountability. (n.d.). *A framework for urban school reform*. Retrieved July 20, 2005, from http://www.nc4ea.org/index .cfm?pg=best_practices&subp=bp_main

National Center for Educational Statistics. (2001). *Educational achievement and black-white inequality*. Washington, DC: U.S. Department of Education, Office of Educational Research and Improvement. Available: http://nces.ed.gov/ pubs2001/2001061A.PDF

Natkin, G., Cooper, B., Fusarelli, L., Alborano, J., Padilla, A., & Ghosh, S. (2002). Myth of the revolving-door superintendency. *School Administrator, 59*(5), 28–31.

Olchefske, J. (2001). *From states to districts: The next phase of the standards-based movement*. Denver, CO: Education Commission of the States. Available: http: //www.ecs.org/ecsmain.asp?page=/html/newsMedia/governancenotes .asp%20%20%20

Pankratz, R. S., & Petrosko, J. M. (Eds.). (2002). *All children can learn: Lessons from the Kentucky reform experience*. San Francisco: Jossey-Bass.

Peterson, P. E., & Campbell, D. (Eds.). (2001). *Charters, vouchers, and public education*. Washington, DC: The Brookings Institution Press.

Phillips, M., Crouse, J., & Ralph, J. (1998). Does the black-white test score gap widen after children enter school? In C. Jencks & M. Phillips (Eds.), *The black-white test score gap* (pp. 229–272). Washington, DC: The Brookings Institution Press.

Powers, V. J. (1998). *Baldrige criteria, partnerships foster culture change across Pinellas district* (Case study). Houston, TX: American Productivity and Quality Center.

Public Education Network. (2004). *About PEN*. Available: http://www.publiceducation .org/home.asp

Quick, H., Birman, B., Gallagher, L., Wolman, J., Chaney, K., & Hikawa, H. (2003). *Evaluation of the blueprint for student success in a standards-based system: Year 2 interim report*. Palo Alto, CA: American Institutes for Research.

Ravitch, D. (2000). *Left back: A century of failed school reforms*. New York: Simon & Schuster.

Ravitch, D., & Vinovskis, M. A. (Eds.). (2000). *Learning from the past: What history teaches us about school reform*. Baltimore, MD: Johns Hopkins University Press.

Resnick, L., & Glennan, T. K., Jr. (2002). Leadership for learning: A theory of action for urban school districts. In A. M. Hightower, M. S. Knapp, J. A. Marsh, & M. W. McLaughlin (Eds.), *School districts and instructional renewal* (pp. 60–72). New York: Teachers College Press.

Rotherham, A. (2001). *Charter school districts: Chester-Upland model.* Washington, DC: Progressive Policy Institute. Available: http://www.ppionline.org/ppi_ci.cfm?contentid=3364&knlgAreaID=110&subsecid=181

Roza, M., & Hawley Miles, K. (2002a). Assessing inequities in school funding within districts: A tool to prepare for student-based budgeting. In School Communities That Work: A National Task Force on the Future of Urban Districts (Ed.), *Portfolio for district redesign.* Providence, RI: Annenberg Institute for School Reform at Brown University.

Roza, M., & Hawley Miles, K. (2002b). First steps to a level playing field: An introduction to student-based budgeting. In School Communities That Work: A National Task Force on the Future of Urban Districts (Ed.), *Portfolio for district redesign.* Providence, RI: Annenberg Institute for School Reform at Brown University.

Roza, M., & Hawley Miles, K. (2002c). Moving toward equity in school funding within districts. In School Communities That Work: A National Task Force on the Future of Urban Districts (Ed.), *Portfolio for district redesign.* Providence, RI: Annenberg Institute for School Reform at Brown University.

Sanders, W. L., & Rivers, J. C. (1996). *Cumulative and residual effects of teachers on future student academic achievement* (Research Progress Report). Knoxville: University of Tennessee Value-Added Research and Assessment Center. Available: file:///C:/WINDOWS/Temporary%20Internet%20Files/Content.IE5/NL4N01TU/981,91,Slide 91

School Communities That Work: A National Task Force on the Future of Urban Districts (Ed.). (2002). *Portfolio for district redesign.* Providence, RI: Annenberg Institute for School Reform at Brown University.

Snipes, J., Doolittle, F., & Herlihy, C. (2002). *Foundations for success: Case studies of how urban school systems improve student achievement.* New York: Manpower Demonstration Research Corporation.

Stone, C. N. (Ed.). (1998). *Changing urban education.* Lawrence: University Press of Kansas.

Supovitz, J., & Taylor, B. S. (2003). *The impact of standard based reform in Duval County, Florida: 1999–2002.* Philadelphia: Consortium for Policy Research in Education.

Swanson, C., & Chaplin, D. (2003). *Counting high school graduates when graduates count: Measuring graduation rates under the high stakes of NCLB.* Washington, DC: Education Policy Center, The Urban Institute.

Teddlie, C., & Reynolds, D. (Eds.). (2000). *The international handbook of school effectiveness research.* New York: Falmer Press.

Thernstrom, A., & Thernstrom, S. (2003). *No excuses: Closing the racial achievement gap in learning.* New York: Simon & Schuster.

Tyack, D. B. (1974). *The one best system: A history of American urban education.* Cambridge, MA: Harvard University Press.

U.S. Census Bureau. (2004). *Projected population of the United States, by race and Hispanic origin: 2000 to 2050.* Available: http://www.census.gov/ipc/www/usinterimproj/natprojtab01a.pdf

Vanourek, G., Finn, C. E., Jr., & Manno, B. V. (2000). Beyond the schoolhouse door: How charter schools are transforming U.S. public education. *Phi Delta Kappan, 81*(10), 736–744.

Wenger, B., Kaye, H. S., & LaPlante, M. (1995). Disabilities among children. *Disability Statistics Abstracts*, No. 15.

Additional Readings

Bogotch, I. E., Brooks, C., MacPhee, B., & Riedlinger, B. (1995). An urban district's knowledge of and attitudes toward school-based innovation, *Urban Education, 30*(1), 5–26.

Cawelti, G., & Protheroe, N. (2003). *High student achievement: How six school districts changed into high performance systems.* Arlington, VA: Educational Research Services.

Cawelti, G., & Protheroe, N. (2003). *Supporting school improvement: Lessons from districts successfully meeting the challenge.* Arlington, VA: Educational Research Services.

Corcoran, T., Fuhrman, S. F., & Belcher, C. (2001). The district role in instructional improvement, *Phi Delta Kappan, 83*(1), 78–84.

Cuban, L., & Usdan, M. (Eds.). (2002). *Powerful reforms with shallow roots: Improving America's urban schools.* New York: Teachers College Press.

David, J., & Shields, P. (2001). *When theory hits reality: Standards-based reform in urban districts.* Arlington, VA: SRI International.

David, J. L. (1990). Restructuring in progress: Lessons from pioneering districts. In R. Elmore et al. (Eds.), *Restructuring schools: The next generation of educational reform* (pp. 209–250). San Francisco: Jossey-Bass.

Elmore, R. F. (1993). The role of local school districts in instructional improvement. In S. Fuhrman (Ed.), *Designing coherent education policy: Improving the system* (pp. 96–124). San Francisco: Jossey-Bass.

Ericson, J., Silverman, D., Berman, P., Nelson, B., & Solomon, D. (2001). *Challenge and opportunity: The impact of charter schools on school districts.* Washington, DC: U.S. Department of Education, Office of Educational Research and Improvement.

Feist, M. (2003). *A web of support: The role of districts in urban middle-grades reform.* Washington, DC: Academy for Educational Development.

Fullan, M. G. (1992). Coordinating school and district development in restructuring. In J. Murphy & F. Hallinger (Eds.), *Restructuring schooling: Learning from ongoing efforts.* Newbury Park, CA: Corwin Press.

Hannaway, J., & Kimball, K. (1998). *Big isn't always bad: School district size, poverty, and standards-based reform.* Washington, DC: Urban Institute.

Harvey, J., McAdams, D., & Hill, P. (2000). *Leaving no child behind: Lessons from the Houston Independent School District.* Houston, TX: Center for Reform of School Systems. Available: http://www.crss.org/Leaving%20ncb.pdf

Hawley Miles, K. (2000). *Matching spending with strategy: Aligning district spending to support a strategy of comprehensive school reform.* District Issues Brief. Washington, DC: New American Schools.

Hawley Miles, K. (2000). *Money matters: Rethinking school and district spending to support comprehensive school reform.* Washington, DC: New American Schools.

Henig, J., & Rich, W. (Eds.). (2002). *Mayors in the middle: Politics, race, and mayoral control of urban schools.* Princeton, NJ: Princeton University Press.

Hill, P. (2001, Winter). Hero worship. *Education Next, 4,* 43–47.

Hirota, J. M., & Jacobs, L. E. (2003). *Vital voices: Building constituencies for public school reform.* Report to the Ford Foundation. New York: Chapin Hall Center for Child Development, Academy for Educational Development.

Holmes, M., Leithwood, K., & Musella, D. (Eds.). (1989). *School systems for effective schools.* Toronto: OISE Press.

Iatarola, P., Stiefel, L., & Schwartz, A. E. (2002). *School performance and resource use: The role of districts in New York City.* New York: New York University, Institute for Education and Social Policy and R. F. Wagner Graduate School of Public Service.

Kearns, D. T., & Harvey, J. (2000). *A legacy of learning: Your stake in standards and new kinds of public schools.* Washington, DC: The Brookings Institution Press.

MacIver, D., & Balfanz, R. (2000). The school district's role in helping high poverty schools become high performing. In B. Gaddy (Ed.), *Including at-risk students in standards-based reform* (pp. 35–69). Aurora, CO: Mid-continent Research for Education and Learning.

Marsh, J. A. (2000). *Connecting districts to the policy dialogue: A review of literature on the relationship of districts with states, schools, and communities.* Seattle, WA: Center for the Study of Teaching and Policy.

Massell, D. (2000). *The district's role in building capacity: Four strategies.* Policy Brief. Philadelphia: Consortium for Policy Research in Education.

Mathews, D. (1996). *Is there a public for public schools?* Dayton, OH: Kettering Foundation Press.

McAdams, D. R. (2000). *Fighting to save our urban schools . . . and winning! Lessons from Houston.* New York: Teachers College Press.

McElroy, M. (2000). *Analysis of alternative school district models.* Seattle: University of Washington, Center on Re-inventing Public Education.

Murphy, J., & Hallinger, P. (1988). Characteristics of instructionally effective districts. *Journal of Educational Research, 81*(3), 175–181.

Ouchi, W. G. (2003). *Making schools work: A revolutionary plan to get your children the education they need.* New York: Simon and Schuster.

Peterson, S. A. (1999). School district central office power and student performance. *School Psychology International, 20*(4), 376–387.

Phenix, D., Siegel, D., Zaltsman, A., & Fruchter, N. (2004). *Virtual district, real improvement: A retrospective evaluation of the Chancellor's District, 1996–2003.* New York: New York University, Institute for Education and Social Policy, Steinhart School of Education.

Ragland, M. A., Asera, R., & Johnson, J. F. (1999). *Urgency, responsibility, efficacy: Preliminary findings of a study of high-performing Texas school districts.* Austin: University of Texas, Charles A. Dana Center.

Simmons, W., & Ucelli, M. (2001, February). *School reform plans should include urban school districts* (Op-Ed.). Available from the Brown University News Bureau: http://www.brown.edu/Administration/News_Bureau/2000-01/00-077.html

Spillane, J. P. (1996). School districts matter: Local educational authorities and state instructional policy, *Educational Policy, 10*(1), 63–87.

Spillane, J. P. (2002). Local theories of teacher change: The pedagogy of district policies and programs, *Teachers College Record, 104*(3), 376–420.

Stringfield, S., & Datnow, A. (1998). Scaling up school restructuring designs in urban schools, *Education and Urban Society, 30*(3), 269–276.

Togneri, W., & Anderson, S. (2003). *Beyond islands of excellence: What districts can do to improve instruction and achievement in all schools.* Washington DC: Learning First Alliance.

Vander Ark, T. (2002). Toward success at scale. *Phi Delta Kappan, 84*(4), 322–326.

Note: This list of readings has been adapted from the School Districts and Educational Improvement Bibliography, available at the School Communities That Work, Annenberg Institute for School Reform at Brown University Web site: http://www.schoolcommunities.org/resources/bibliography.html

Index

About the Author

DONALD R. MCADAMS is president of the Center for Reform of School Systems. In 2002 he completed 12 years as a board member of the Houston Independent School District, serving twice as board president. He is a former university professor, college president, and quality management consultant. He holds a PhD from Duke University in British history and is the author of *Fighting to Save Our Urban Schools . . . and Winning! Lessons from Houston.*